THE EVOLUTION OF CHRISTIANITY

SERIES IN AMERICAN STUDIES

Editor-in-Chief: Joseph J. Kwiat
PROGRAM IN AMERICAN STUDIES
UNIVERSITY OF MINNESOTA

THE EVOLUTION OF

CHRISTIANITY

By

LYMAN ABBOTT

With a New Introduction by
JOHN A. DE JONG
DEPARTMENT OF HISTORY
CENTRAL COLLEGE, PELLA, IOWA

JOHNSON REPRINT CORPORATION

New York and London

1969

The edition reproduced here was originally
published in 1892.

Library of Congress Catalog Card Number: 72-80040

Printed in the U. S. A.

INTRODUCTION

In one of his famous sermons on evolution, Henry Ward Beecher, Lyman Abbott's illustrious predecessor in the Plymouth Congregational Church of Brooklyn, preached that acceptance of the idea of evolution must inevitably bring with it a reconstruction in theology. Apparently to reassure those to whom the idea of theological reconstruction was even more disturbing than acceptance of evolution, Beecher proceeded to explain that this was something to be welcomed rather than feared. It would, he claimed, serve to give to Christian beliefs "a breadth and certainty not possible in their present philosophical condition."[1] Following Beecher, Lyman Abbott enthusiastically devoted a substantial part of his career as preacher, editor, and author to the task of bending evolutionary thought to the service of theological reconstruction, sharing with Beecher the hope that it would give new relevance and vitality to the Christian faith and at the same time help to rid it of some of its archaic encumbrances.

The movement of theological reconstruction in which both Beecher and Abbott joined was known to them and their contemporaries as the New Theology. It was an attempt to bring Chris-

---

[1] Henry Ward Beecher, *Evolution and Religion* (New York, 1885), p. 53.

v

tian thought into harmony with the latest in science, philosophy, theology, the higher criticism of the Bible, and cultural values in the last decades of the nineteenth century. Some of its characteristic features were belief in the immanence of a benevolent God, emphasis on Christ as a revealer of God, advocacy of a moral influence theory of the atonement, a concern for social justice, and a more optimistic view of man's moral potential than had been characteristic of strict Calvinism. In all of this the formulators of the New Theology were determined not only to preserve but also to revitalize the essentials of traditional Christianity with its emphasis on revelation, the work of Christ, sin, and redemption. Because of this conscious striving to combine modernity with orthodoxy, students of the New Theology have aptly renamed it "evangelical" or "Christocentric" liberalism.[2]

Although Darwinian evolution was one of the most important catalysts of the New Theology, its impact was not unique but rather representative of and supplementary to other influences that were broader in scope and reached further

---

[2] Kenneth Cauthen, *The Impact of American Religious Liberalism* (New York, 1962), pp. 41–146; H. Shelton Smith, "The Christocentric Liberal Tradition," in *American Christianity: An Historical Interpretation with Representative Documents,* ed. H. S. Smith, R. T. Handy, and L. A. Loetscher (2 vols.; New York, 1961), II, 255–65.

back into time. These included the rationalism and humanism of the Enlightenment, the romantic idealism of the nineteenth century, the growth of democratic ideals and institutions, and nineteenth-century man's optimistic faith in progress. The power and persuasiveness of these inherently attractive cultural forces were greatly enhanced when they were viewed in the light of American history with its material prosperity and security, its progress in the practice of democracy, and its pre-Civil war reform movements that reflected both moral fervor and confidence in man. On the basis of this experience, the hope that man might achieve social and individual perfection did not seem so wild a dream after all.

Even a most cursory glance at the implications of these ideals and hopes indicates why many nineteenth-century American churchmen felt the need for theological revision. At any number of points threats existed to basic Christian doctrines. Science-inspired rationalism, for example, encouraged so profound a respect for the autonomy of human reason that for many the claims of supernatural revelation were inevitably weakened. Romantic intuitionism further encouraged this. Modern science's picture of the universe under the dominion of natural law made belief in miracles increasingly difficult. Nineteenth-century indications of social progress made it easy for some to dream that man's highest ideals could be realized in this life rather than in the one to come. And finally, the Calvinistic emphasis on original sin, total depravity, total dependence on grace, divine election, and eternal damnation became increasingly difficult to reconcile with the humanistic optimism of the day. Many American churchmen were sensitive to these difficulties, for sensitivity to cultural changes had become an essential ingredient of survival in a society that practiced separation of church and state and featured extensive denominational competition. But survival was not their only concern. The major Protestant denominations in the United States were also bent on exercising a major influence in the building of a Christian society — a society that was thoroughly infused with and guided by Christian values. If they were to influence and lead free men, the churches had to work with the cultural forces of the day and not place themselves too obviously in opposition to them. Not surprisingly, therefore, American churches displayed a readiness to embrace the dominant social and cultural movements in nineteenth-century America and invest them with a Christian purpose when they could do so without compromising the faith. Many even succeeded in detecting in such things as the growth of American democracy or the security and prosperity of the nation evidence that their religious goals for America were about to be realized.

As one would expect in view of the free and open pattern of religious life in America, the responses to the new and sometimes upsetting cultural forces varied. In Universalism, Unitarianism, and Transcendentalism one finds the most radical breaks with what had apparently become an outmoded Calvinism. The pietism, perfectionism, and millennialism of nineteenth-century evangelical Protestantism represented adjustments more within the bounds of traditional Christian experience. Even in those denominations where Calvinism remained a dominant force, significant concessions were made to the new spirit of the age. In response to the increasing prestige of science and confidence in human reason, natural theology received greater attention than ever before. Although few envisioned that divine revelation could ever be dispensed with, there was increased confidence in man's ability to find evidence of God's existence and to gain insight into his attributes in the designed structure and orderly operation of the universe. In addition, a number of Calvinistic theologians displayed a willingness to question, modify, and restate the traditional doctrines of depravity, predestination, free will, eternal damnation, and others. Horace Bushnell offered some of the most exciting revisions of Calvinistic theology by boldly embracing romantic intuitionism and by offering fresh views of Christology, the atonement, and the nature of religious experience. His analysis of language served to stimulate new attitudes toward creeds and doctrinal formulations. Bushnell's pioneering theological speculations clearly indicated that the groundwork for a major theological reconstruction had been laid before the appearance of Darwin's theory of evolution.

The most important effect of the idea of evolution was to hasten the pace of theological reconstruction. In part this was due to the fact that it threatened several articles of belief, particularly those concerning revelation, creation, and human sin. But it also strengthened the ideals of rationalism, humanism, and optimism already at work in reshaping American culture. For some thinkers this merely added to the general distress that the idea of evolution caused, but one need not read extensively in the literature of the New Theology to discover that its exponents regarded evolution as something more than a troublesome idea to be confronted from a purely defensive posture. Like Beecher, they viewed it as an idea that could be exploited to provide impressive intellectual support for some of the important new trends in theology. The New Theology would undoubtedly have emerged without the impetus provided by evolutionary thought, for its essential features were in the process of formation before the idea of evolution gained general acceptance; but at each point where modifications of Protestant thought were already underway to bring it into harmony with the rationalistic, humanistic, and optimistic values of the age, it was possible to marshal the support of evolution. A case in point was the doctrine of God's immanence in nature, one of the central concepts in the New Theology. Although the idea of evolution was a major influence in the development of this doctrine, romantic idealism and nineteenth-century faith in progress were already inspiring it among religious thinkers when evolution became a major intellectual force. In each case of parallel influence of this sort, the extent to which evolution was the main factor causing doctrinal revision or the extent to which it simply served to support revisions already in progress is difficult to determine. In any event, regardless of how one assigns priority of influence, the major outlines of the New Theology were clearly visible by the decade of the 1880's.

The place of Lyman Abbott in this process of theological reconstruction was somewhat ambiguous. By his own admission, he was not an original or particularly deep thinker; and his work reflects this. It is difficult, therefore, to credit him with any substantial innovations in the New

Theology. Nor does one find in his writings a particularly profound or searching analysis of the New Theology. For these qualities one must consult the writings of other theologians in the movement such as Theodore T. Munger, Egbert C. Smyth and his brother Newman Smyth, William Adams Brown, William N. Clarke, Henry Churchill King, and George A. Gordon. But as a skilled popularizer and defender of the New Theology in lucid and graceful prose that was both appealing and readily accessible to all types of readers, Abbott had few peers. Perhaps because he was not an original or particularly deep thinker he is all the more valuable a source for viewing the New Theology in its broadest if not its deepest dimensions.

Abbott's emergence as one of the foremost expositors of the New Theology was gradual. When he began his ministry in 1860 after leaving a promising law career, his theology was conservative and evangelical. His books, editorials, and reviews from the first years of his ministry reflected a straightforward, unsophisticated, and uncritical acceptance of the Bible as a literally inspired book whose claims for itself were to be taken at face value. The Gospels, for example, were an "authentic narrative" and sufficient grounds for accepting both the events and miracles of Christ's life. Doctrinally he accepted the fall of Adam, the inheritance of Adam's sin by all, and a sacrificial theory of the atonement. His outlook was not narrowly denominational but tolerant and catholic, qualities that he retained throughout his life. He was, however, strongly opposed to radical tendencies in theology. In reviews and editorials in the *Illustrated Christian Weekly,* which he edited in the early 1870's, he criticized such movements as the free religion of Francis E. Abbot and the religion of humanity of Octavius B. Frothingham. He also rejected most of the results of critical Biblical scholarship that he was later to accept. In 1876 Abbott left the editorship of the *Illustrated Christian Weekly* to join Henry Ward Beecher's *Christian Union.* He eventually became chief editor of the journal and subsequently changed its name to the *Outlook.* Under the influence of Beecher and of continued theological study, Abbott's religious position changed. He gave up the literal accuracy of the Bible and in time became one of the foremost supporters of liberal theology among Congregationalists. By 1890 he was prepared to attempt an ambitious exposition of the New Theology in which the application of evolution to religion was a central theme.[3]

According to his own account of how he became an evolutionist, Abbott had little difficulty

---

[3] Ira V. Brown, *Lyman Abbott, Christian Evolutionist: A Study in Religious Liberalism* (Cambridge, Mass., 1953), pp. 55–78.

reconciling the idea with his religious beliefs. Since he professed no competence in science and claimed no authority for the Bible on scientific matters, it was relatively easy for him to be swayed by the nearly universal acceptance of evolution among scientists and other intellectual authorities. Abbott disposed of the fear that evolutionary theory encouraged atheism by insisting that it was neutral with respect to that question. Evolution described a natural process but did not throw light on the causes that initiated the process or operated to maintain it. Evolution, to be sure, could be interpreted atheistically, but there was little doubt in Abbott's mind that a theistic interpretation was thoroughly consistent with scientific evidence. Abbott also easily disposed of the problems that the theory of natural selection, with its implications of struggle, posed for the concept of a designed universe and the maintenance of ethical standards. Natural selection was only one among several possible explanations of the evolutionary process and at best could only be a partial explanation. Since even among scientists the extent to which natural selection explained evolution was an open question, Abbott's position could be supported with appeals to scientific testimony. But the most important factor in Abbott's easy acceptance of evolution was his adoption of the broadest possible definition of the concept. Following John

Fiske, Henry L. Drummond, Beecher, and others, he equated evolution with progressive development. Practically speaking he made no distinction between evolution and historical change. The definition he used most consistently was that of the geologist, Joseph Le Conte, who held evolution to be "continuous progressive change, according to certain laws, and by means of resident forces." This was such a broad interpretation that one could do with it much as one pleased. Whatever disturbing thoughts "resident forces" may have suggested to others, Abbott removed them by simply identifying these forces with the action of God immanent in nature. The applications of the idea of divine immanence in the thought of Abbott and other liberals concerned with reconciling religion and evolution almost defy description. With one stroke the force of the mechanistic materialism suggested in evolutionary theory and many other areas of nineteenth-century science was blunted. Given the doctrine of immanence there was literally no scientific discovery respecting the processes of nature that could harm religious faith. Moreover, the doctrine of immanence allowed for an easy retention of belief in miracles and divine providence. In fact, it very nearly abolished the distinction between the natural and the supernatural. Fortified by this assurance Abbott dispensed with intricate exercises in the reconciliation of evolution and religion and moved on to the more important task of applying the idea of evolution to the exposition of religious truth. Further encouraging him in this was the conviction, derived in part from the doctrine of immanence, that natural and spiritual laws were so closely related and so similar in character that the former, for example, the law of evolution, could be used to illustrate and interpret the latter.

The Evolution of Christianity, published in 1892, was the first detailed presentation of Abbott's mature views on the application of evolution to religion. It applied the idea to the Bible, theological development, church history, social progress, and the religious life of the individual soul. He followed it with *Christianity and Social Problems* (1896), a book not explicitly concerned with evolutionary thought but obviously based on the idea of Christianity as a factor in social evolution. In *The Theology of an Evolutionist* (1897) Abbott explored evolutionary interpretations of a number of Christian doctrines, including revelation, Christology, sin, redemption, miracles, and immortality. *The Life and Letters of Paul the Apostle* (1898) viewed the evolution of Paul's thought. Finally, in 1901, Abbott published *The Life and Literature of the Ancient Hebrews,* a book expressing total acceptance of the higher criticism of the Bible, which he believed was closely related to evolutionary thought. Taken as a whole these books provided a comprehensive overview of the New Theology, and chapter four of *The Evolution of Christianity* presented a remarkably compact statement of its main characteristics and a recognition of the religious and cultural influences that entered into its formation.

Viewing Abbott's work purely from the standpoint of his application of the idea of evolution, one must take some exception to his claim that he was a radical evolutionist. He rested this claim on his willingness to apply the concept of evolution to all facets of religious thought and experience. To an extent he did this, mainly by showing how the Christian life embraced a number of evolutionary processes. Revelation, for example, took place through evolution and so did the experience of salvation. The church and theology also evolved. These characteristics had been apparent to religious thinkers before Darwin, but according to Abbott the theory of evolution enabled modern man to see them with greater clarity than before. Although in all of this the idea of evolution inspired some new insights, the term was used so broadly that it lost precise meaning as a scientific or philosophic concept. But even more damaging to Abbott's claim to a radical application of the idea of evolution was his use of it almost solely for apologetic purposes. He as much as admitted this in the Preface to *The Evolution of Christianity* where he specifically stated that his intent was not to discover new religious truths but "to show that the historic faith of Christendom, when stated in terms of evolutionary philosophy, is not only preserved, but is so cleansed of pagan thought and feeling, as to be presented in a purer and more powerful form." Such a use of the idea of evolution might indeed result in a universal application of the idea, but it could hardly lead to anything very radical. And its likelihood of leading to anything radical was further reduced by Abbott's conception of the essential nature of the Christian religion. For although he recognized that Christianity embraced evolutionary processes of various types and that the concept of evolution lent itself to the exposition of a number of Christian beliefs, Abbott could find no place for evolution at the very core of the Christian religion.

Christianity's fundamental immunity to evolution is seen most clearly in the distinction that Abbott drew between theology and religion. There was nothing particularly unique about this distinction; religious thinkers had frequently employed it in one form or another. In Abbott's time it expressed a widespread reaction against the emphasis on creeds and dogma that many feared had characterized too much of Christian practice in the past, especially among Calvinists. It was also an indication of how vulnerable creeds and theological formulas had become in the face of critical, science-oriented rationalism. Religion interpreted as experience rather than belief was, of course, far less vulnerable to this sort of criticism. Recognizing this, Abbott insisted that religion was largely spiritual, consisting of an experienced relationship between God and man that produced fruits in man-to-man relationships as well. As revealed in the Bible in the life of the Hebrews and the teachings of Christ, the distinguishing marks of true religion were faith, hope, love, and humility. True religion defined in this way did not change. Theology, on the other hand, was the effort of man to explain, interpret, and rationalize religion. In theology there was change, and it was possible for a theology to define and express religious experience with varying degrees of clarity and fidelity to its deepest essence. In short, theology evolved as men acquired more elevated insights into the nature of God, worship, and righteousness. Thus Abbott was confident that nineteenth-century Christianity was far superior to that of earlier centuries just as the Christianity of the future would be superior to that of the nineteenth century. But this was not due to any change in the nature of true religion but rather was due to the evolution of a purer

and more consistent understanding and application of the religion taught in its perfection by
Christ. Beyond Christ's pure religion there could
be no evolution. At best this was only superficially an application of the concept of evolution
and was only slightly more consistent with historical experience or the generalized law of progress to which Abbott professed to be a radical
adherent.

One may make similar observations concerning Abbott's application of the idea of evolution
to the church, revelation, Jesus, and finally God.
It is interesting that in his discussion of Jesus,
Abbott came the closest to admitting that he was
not applying evolution as radically as he might
have. Here he considered the idea that a thoroughly radical application would necessitate
believing that Christ was a product of evolution
and that there could be evolutionary progress
beyond him. But this Abbott could not accept.
Christ was a causal force behind evolution and
therefore could not be subject to it. Furthermore,
beyond perfection there could be no evolution.
But what was unthinkable to Abbott was not
unthinkable to others, particularly those who,
under the influence of emergent theories of evolution, were willing to apply the concept to God
himself.[4]

---

[4] Frank H. Foster, *The Modern Movement in American
Theology* (New York, 1939), pp. 210–211.

Whether Abbott's less than radical application of the idea of evolution constituted a strength or weakness will vary with the concerns of the critic. Because he took what may be described as the middle ground in his exposition of both the idea of evolution and the New Theology, he was open to and received criticism from both ends of the theological spectrum.[5] And yet, his moderate, restrained approach was undoubtedly a major cause of his success in becoming one of the most influential exponents of liberal theology in his day.

In seeking other factors in Abbott's success one must give major consideration to his extraordinary ability to give theological expression to the dominant cultural values of his age, particularly the values of that class of liberal thinking American Protestants that constituted his largest audience. It is not difficult to delineate those qualities of Abbott's preaching and writing that marked his success among these people and enabled him to present them with a renewed and revitalized conception of the Christian faith. Abbott's respect for reason was one of the foremost of these qualities; but one may also note his nondogmatic and tolerant attitude, his passion for liberty and social justice, his sensitivity to the optimism of the times, and his concern for more

---

[5] Brown, *Abbott*, pp. 143–149.

refined and more humane conceptions of those doctrines that in their Calvinistic form had become intellectually and morally repulsive to many. However, probably nothing contributed more to the general appeal of his work than his ability to incorporate into it the democratic and humanistic values of the day. His interpretation of Christianity as the foe of authoritarianism in all its forms and the champion of the right of individual judgment, faith in man's capacity for self-government, and the improvement of society was a well-calculated appeal to the highest aspirations of his audience. The New Theology was, if nothing more, a democratic theology, and in Abbott's hands it frankly and unashamedly glorified man.

It was at this point that the doctrine of divine immanence once again performed a vital service for Abbott, allowing him to incorporate the prevailing cultural forces into his theology in much the same way it had facilitated the incorporation of evolution into Christian thought. Undoubtedly the most startling use of the doctrine of immanence for this end was its application to man. Abbott saw God in man just as in nature, except, of course, for those differences necessary to protect man's freedom of will and action. From this Abbott concluded that the only difference between God's incarnation in Christ and his immanence in man was one of degree. In the final analysis "man and God are in very essence one." In this way Abbott discovered implications in the idea of divine immanence that an earlier generation of Congregationalists had branded heresy when expressed in the works of Ralph Waldo Emerson and Theodore Parker. Further reminiscent of Transcendentalism, and more immediately of Bushnell, was Abbott's contention that God's immanence in man necessarily implied intuitionism. Again with true insight into the spirit of his day, Abbott recognized in intuitionism a corrective to the authoritarian dogmatism that in his opinion had for too long plagued Protestantism. When one notes how thoroughly Abbott sought to incorporate into his exposition of the New Theology the most popular cultural values of his time, one can hardly fail to assign to rationalism and humanistic optimism a larger and more influential role than evolution in Abbott's reconstruction of theology.

Contemporary students of the New Theology still find much to admire in this successful accommodation of Christianity to nineteenth-century culture, but they also find in it a cause for some concern. And so they have frequently charged that in achieving their success, Abbott and his fellow liberals compromised, or worse, surrendered, the other goal of the New Theology, which was fidelity to traditional Christian faith. Consequently what remained after the work of reconstruction was completed was not a purified and revitalized Christianity but a religion of culture that was only superficially Christian. Although in Abbott's case surrender would be too strong a term, it is nonetheless possible to recognize in *The Evolution of Christianity* and similar works many of the characteristics of what H. R. Niebuhr has defined as "cultural Christianity."[6] An obvious example was Abbott's description of Christianity as the primary agent in the realization of some of the most cherished values and institutions of nineteenth-century Americans. In fact, it is frequently difficult to determine whether Abbott saw Christianity realized in democratic institutions or democratic institutions realized in Christianity. This was particularly apparent in his discussion of the evolution of society in which he for all practical purposes attributed social progress to the influence of Christianity. At the same time, his interpretations of the life and teachings of Christ bore the stamp of nineteenth-century values. Jesus preached essentially nineteenth-century concepts of faith in man, the progressive character of history, and social justice. Although the faithfulness of these interpretations to Christ's actual teachings has come to be questioned, there is little doubt that these elements

[6] H. R. Niebuhr, *Christ and Culture* (New York, 1951), Chapter III.

of humanism and social concern still find a sympathetic response among twentieth-century churchmen. Greater concern has centered on the inadequate conception of human sin and the superficial treatment of the problem of evil that generally characterized the New Theology. Abbott's handling of these themes illuminates this concern. In accepting the idea of evolution he indicated that his greatest difficulties were encountered in reconciling evolution with the Genesis account of the origin of sin. Evolution implied that man was a creature who was rising from lower animal origins and not a creature that had fallen from a state of original perfection. Critical rereading of the Bible in the light of the higher criticism enabled Abbott to accept the implications of the evolutionary account of man's beginnings and also to revise his evangelical notions on the origin and nature of sin. But in rejecting a literal reading of the Biblical story of the Fall, Abbott also apparently dropped part of the message that Christians had traditionally drawn from that story, particularly the notion that pride and rebellion were at the basis of human sin. His thinking finally came to rest in an evolutionary conception of sin that made it simply a matter of reversion to man's animal past. Sin was man yielding to the enticements of his lower animal nature. Abbott did not go so far as to dismiss sin as mere immaturity or lack of development. Men knew better and were guilty of deliberate disobedience. But the general drift of his thought was to regard this as a weakness and not the manifestation of a persistent inclination toward pride and self-serving. Twentieth-century theologians, Reinhold Niebuhr most notably, have found these views to be excessively optimistic as well as false to the deepest Biblical insights into human nature. But however inadequate they may have come to appear to a later generation of religious thinkers, they accurately reflected the optimism of Abbott's generation as it responded to the idea of evolution and the force of moral idealism.

Another facet of Abbott's theology that has come to be seen in a different light because of differences in the experiences of his generation and those that followed was his approach to the perennial problem of the nature of faith. Abbott did not treat this problem explicitly in *The Evolution of Christianity*, but one can nevertheless detect in his writing a deliberate effort to picture belief as something easy, natural, and attractive for his contemporaries. He achieved this principally by showing that history, science, and human experience generally confirmed the essential claims and teachings of Christianity. Thus faith in Christ emerged as something not too dramatically different from faith in those cultural values and institutions that nineteenth-century Americans to a large extent already believed in. This treatment was not entirely foreign to the history of Christian thought, but Abbott's implied recommendation of the Christian faith on the grounds of its congruity with the latest in man's wisdom represented a significant departure from the view that the Christian faith was something to be grasped despite its appearance as foolishness before the wisdom of the world — a view to which some of the more evangelical of Abbott's contemporaries still clung. But perhaps more significant than this departure was the probability that a faith tied as closely as Abbott's was to nineteenth-century experiences and values ran the exceedingly grave danger of becoming discredited and inaccessible to men in the face of changed historical circumstances. This was to be dramatically illustrated in the twentieth century as events worked to convince large numbers of thoughtful and concerned persons that history is not progressive, that man is not gradually casting off the vestiges of an animal past, and that reason, justice, and righteousness do not inevitably triumph.

To later generations brought up under the full impact of these sobering conclusions, the optimistic, liberal theology of Lyman Abbott came to have increasingly less to say. This is not to suggest that Abbott's theology, because it reflected so clearly late nineteenth-century thought, contained flaws not shared by other religious thinkers. The theology of Reinhold Niebuhr, for example, which for many came to speak with more relevance than Abbott's in the middle of the twentieth century, was as certainly conditioned by historical experience as was Abbott's. Perhaps this does no more than illustrate once again the truism that Christian thought has and always will be conditioned by its cultural environment. Although much more might be said about *The Evolution of Christianity* than that it was a reflection of its age, one would have to search long for a work that did this more faithfully than Abbott's.

John A. De Jong

SELECT BIBLIOGRAPHY

I. Works by Lyman Abbott

Christianity and Social Problems. Boston, 1896.

The Evolution of Christianity. Boston, 1892.

Henry Ward Beecher. Boston, 1903.

In Aid of Faith. New York, 1886.

The Life and Letters of Paul the Apostle. Boston, 1898.

The Life and Literature of the Ancient Hebrews. Boston, 1901.

Reminiscences. Boston, 1915.

The Theology of an Evolutionist. Boston, 1897.

II. Secondary Accounts

Brown, Ira. *Lyman Abbott, Christian Evolutionist: A Study in Religious Liberalism.* Cambridge, Mass., 1953.

Cauthen, Kenneth. *The Impact of American Religious Liberalism.* New York, 1962.

Foster, Frank H. *The Modern Movement in American Theology.* New York, 1939.

Persons, Stow. "Evolution and Theology," in *Evolutionary Thought in America,* ed. S. Persons. New York, 1956. Pp. 422–53.

Persons, Stow. "Religion and Modernity," *The Shaping of American Religion,* Vol. I of *Religion in American Life,* ed. James Ward Smith and A. Leland Jamison. 4 vols. Princeton, N. J., 1961. Pp. 369–401.

Smith, H. Shelton. "The Christocentric Liberal Tradition," in *American Christianity: An Historical Interpretation with Representative Documents,* ed. H. S. Smith, R. T. Handy, and L. A. Loetscher. 2 vols. New York, 1963. Vol. II, pp. 255–308.

Williams, Daniel D. *The Andover Liberals: A Study in American Theology.* New York, 1941.

THE EVOLUTION OF
CHRISTIANITY

BY

LYMAN ABBOTT

BOSTON AND NEW YORK
HOUGHTON, MIFFLIN AND COMPANY
The Riverside Press, Cambridge
1892

PREFACE.

WE are living in a time of religious ferment. What shall we do? Attempt to keep the new wine in the old bottles? That can only end in destroying the bottles and spilling the wine. Attempt to stop the fermentation? Impossible! And if possible, the only result would be to spoil the wine. No! Put the new wine into new bottles, that both may be preserved. Spiritual experience is always new. It must therefore find a new expression in each age. This book is an attempt to restate the eternal yet ever new truths of the religious life in the terms of modern philosophic thought.

The teachers in the modern church may be divided into three parties: one is endeavoring to defend the faith of the fathers and the forms in which that faith was expressed; one repudiates both the faith and the forms; one holds fast to the faith, but endeavors to restate it in forms more rational and more consistent with modern habits of thought. To confound the second and third of these parties, because they agree in discarding ancient formularies, is a natural but a very radical blunder. The New Theology does not tend toward unfaith; it is, on the contrary, an endeavor to maintain faith by expressing it in terms which are more intelligible and credible. I hope that the reader of these pages will discover that I have not abandoned the historic faith of Christendom to become an evolutionist, but have endeavored to show that the historic faith of Christendom, when stated in the terms of an evolutionary philosophy, is not only preserved, but is so cleansed of pagan thought and feeling, as to be presented in a purer and more powerful form.

Mr. Drummond has contended, not that there is an analogy between natural and spiritual laws, but that the natural and the spiritual belong to one kingdom, so that the natural laws are projected into the spiritual world. It is my endeavor in this volume, in like manner, not to trace an analogy between evolution in the physical realm, and progress in the spiritual realm, but to show that the law of progress is the same in both. In the spiritual, as in the physical, God is the secret and source of life; phenomena, whether material or spiritual, are the manifestation of his presence; but he manifests himself in growth, not in stereotyped and stationary forms; and this growth is from lower to higher, from simpler to more complex forms, according to well defined and invariable laws, and by a force resident in the growing object itself. That unknown force is God — God in nature, God in the church, God in society, and God in the individual soul. The only cognizable difference between evolution in the physical and evolution in the spiritual realms is that nature cannot shut God out, nor hinder his working, nor disregard the laws of its own life; but man can and does. These principles constitute, to borrow a musical phrase, the *motif* of this book.

The chapters which constitute the book were originally delivered, extemporaneously, as lectures before the Lowell Institute of Boston. After their delivery their publication was called for. They had not been reported in full, and compliance with the request for their publication necessitated writing them. In some instances criticism showed that I had failed to make my meaning clear. In such cases I have modified my original statements. But this has been done only for the purpose of avoiding misapprehension, not because in any case I have thought it prudent to modify the opinions expressed. I have not hesitated to incorporate in the book, as in the lectures, the substance, and in some cases the phraseology, of previous periodical publications ; chapter fourth is to a considerable extent such a modification of matter previously printed.

To some readers the chapter on the Evolution of the Bible, and that on the Evolution of the Soul, may seem to surrender vital and essential articles of Christian faith. I hope to others they will make all that is vital in the faith of the church concerning justification, sin, and redemption more rational and credible. My aim has been, not to destroy, but to reconstruct.

LYMAN ABBOTT.

BROOKLYN, N. Y., *May,* 1892.

CONTENTS.

THE
EVOLUTION OF CHRISTIANITY.

CHAPTER I.

EVOLUTION AND RELIGION.

EVOLUTION is defined by Professor Le Conte as "continuous progressive change, according to certain laws, and by means of resident forces." Religion has been defined by an English divine as "the life of God in the soul of man." It is my object to show that the Christian religion is itself an evolution; that is, that this life of God in humanity is one of continuous progressive change, according to certain divine laws, and by means of forces, or a force, resident in humanity. The proposition is a very simple one; illustrated and applied, it may help to solve some of the problems which are perplexing us concerning the Bible, the church, theology, social ethics, and spiritual experience.

All scientific men to-day are evolutionists. That is, they agree substantially in holding that all life proceeds, by a regular and orderly sequence, from simple to more complex forms, from lower to higher forms, and in accordance with laws which either now are or may yet be understood, or are at all events a proper subject of hopeful investigation. The truth of this doctrine I assume; that is, I assume that all life, including the religious life, proceeds by a regular and orderly sequence from simple and lower forms to more complex and higher forms, in institutions, in thought, in practical conduct, and in spiritual experience. It is my purpose not so much to demonstrate this proposition as to state, exemplify, and apply it.

As "evolution" is the latest word of science, so "life" is the supreme word of religion. All religious men agree that there is a life of God in the soul of man. Max Müller suggests a more scientific definition of religion, — but the two are identical in sense, though different in form. He says that "religion consists in the perception of the Infinite under such manifestations as are able to influence the moral character of man." [1] The Christian religion, then, is the perception of that manifestation of God, historically made in and through Jesus Christ, which has produced the changes in the moral life of man whose aggregate result is seen in the complex life of Christendom, past and present. As

[1] *Natural Religion*, p. 188.

all scientific men believe in evolution, — the orderly development of life from lower to higher forms, — so all Christians believe that there has been a manifestation of God in Jesus Christ which has produced historical Christianity. As I assume the truth of evolution, so I assume the truth of this fundamental article of the Christian faith. With the scientific believer, I believe in the orderly and progressive development of all life; with the religious believer, I believe in the reality of a life of God in the soul of man. It is not my object to reconcile these two beliefs, but, assuming the truth of both, to show that this divine life is itself subject to the law of all life; that Christianity is itself an evolution. Applying this law to the history of the Christian religion, it is my object to show that the manifestation of God in Jesus Christ has been a gradual and growing manifestation, and that the changes wrought thereby in the moral life of man have been gradual and growing changes, wrought by spiritual forces, or a spiritual force, resident in man.

There are in Professor Le Conte's definition of evolution three terms. Evolution is *first* a continuous progressive change; *second*, according to certain laws; *third*, by means of resident forces. Each of these elements enters into and characterizes the development of Christianity.

Christianity has been, not a fixed and unchanging factor, but a life, subject to a continuous progressive change; this change has been, not lawless, irregular, and unaccountable, but according to certain laws, which, though by no means well understood, have never been either suspended or violated; and the cause of this change, or these changes, has been a force, not foreign to man himself, but residing in him. Thus Christianity, whether regarded as an institutional, an intellectual, a social, or a moral life, has exemplified the law of evolution.

A few more words of exact definition are needed, for it cannot be doubted that in the discussion concerning the relation of Christianity to evolution — or in the larger and less exact phrase, concerning the relation of theology to science — there has been much ignorance and more prejudice: on the part of theological experts, ignorance respecting the true nature of evolution; on the part of scientific experts, ignorance respecting the true nature of religion. The theological discussions of our time grow out of an attempt, on the one hand, to restate the principles of the Christian life in terms of an evolutionary philosophy, or in terms consistent with that philosophy; and, on the other hand, out of resistance to this attempt, either by denying evolutionary philosophy altogether, or by main-

taining that the Christian religion is an exception
to the ordinary laws of life: that it is not and
cannot be a continuous progression, but is and
must be always unchanging; that it is not governed by certain laws, certainly not by laws
which man can understand, but is dependent on
the inscrutable if not capricious will of an unknown Person; that it has its operating causes,
not in a force or forces resident in humanity,
but in a force or forces outside humanity. As
I have said, I do not propose to discuss this
question, except as an attempt to restate the
principles of the Christian life in the terms of
an evolutionary philosophy is such a discussion;
but it is evident, if such a restatement is to be
made, that we must understand at the outset
what we mean both by evolution and by the
Christian life.

The doctrine of evolution, then, makes no attempt whatever to explain the nature or origin
of life. It is concerned, not with the origin,
but with the phenomena of life. It sees the
forces resident in the phenomena, but it throws
no light on the question how they came there.
It traces the tree from the seed, the animal
from the embryo, the planetary system from
its nebulous condition; it investigates and as-
certains the process of development: but it does
not explain, or offer to explain, what is the

difference between the seed which is a living thing and the grain of sand which is dead, or between the vitalized and the unvitalized egg, or what there is in the nebulæ which produces out of chaos a beautiful world fitted for human habitation. One may with Haeckel believe in spontaneous generation, or with Tyndall disbelieve in it, and in either case be an evolutionist. Evolution traces only the processes of life; it does not offer to explain the nature or the origin of life. Life antedates all progress; and evolution only traces progress. The evolutionary theologian, then, must believe that the spiritual life shows itself in a continuous progress according to an orderly and regular sequence; but his belief in evolution will throw no light whatever on the question as to the secret of that life which antedates spiritual progress. He must believe that this spiritual force is resident in humanity; but how it came to be resident in humanity, evolution cannot tell him. This he must learn, if at all, elsewhere.

Making no attempt to explain the origin of life, the evolutionist insists that the processes of life are always from the simple to the complex: from the simple nebulæ to the complicated world containing mineral substances and vegetable and animal life; from the germinant mollusk through every form of animate creation up to the vertebrate mammal, including man; from the family, through the tribe, to the nation; from the paternal form of government, through the oligarchic and the aristocratic, to the democratic; from slavery, — the patriarchal capitalist owning his slave on terms hardly different from those on which he owns his wife, — to the complicated relationship of modern society between employer and employed. In this movement, notwithstanding apparent blunders, false types and arrested developments, the evolutionist sees a steady progress from lower to higher forms of life. The Christian evolutionist, then, will expect to find modern Christianity more complex than primitive Christianity. For the purpose of this comparison, I do not go back of Bethlehem: then, the confession "Thou art the Christ, the Son of the Living God," — now, the Episcopal Thirty-nine Articles, the Methodist Episcopal Twenty-four Articles, or the Westminster Confession of Faith of Thirty-three Chapters, with their numerous sub-sections; then, the simple supper-talk with the twelve friends, met in a fellowship sanctified by prayer and love — now, an elaborate altar, jeweled vestments, pealing organ, kneeling and awe-stricken worshipers; then, meetings from house to house for prayer, Christian praise, and instruction in the simpler facts of the Master's life and the fundamental principles of his kingdom, — now, churches, with preachers, elders, bishops, sessions, presbyteries, councils, associations, missionary boards; then, a brief prayer, breathing the common wants of universal humanity in a few simple petitions, — now, an elaborate ritual, appealing to ear and eye and imagination, by all the accessories which art and music and historic association combined can confer; then, a brotherhood in Jerusalem, with all things in common, and a board of deacons to see that all were fed and none were surfeited, — now, a brotherly love making its way, in spite of selfishness, towards the realization of that brotherhood of humanity which is as yet only a dream of poets. And he will expect to find that the Christianity of the nineteenth century, despite its failures and defects, is better, intellectually, organically, morally, and spiritually, than the Christianity of the first century.

The doctrine of evolution is not a doctrine of harmonious and uninterrupted progress. The most common, if not the most accurate formula of evolution is "struggle for existence, survival of the fittest." The doctrine of evolution assumes that there are forces in the world seemingly hostile to progress, that life is a perpetual battle and progress a perpetual victory. The Christian evolutionist will then expect to find

Christianity a warfare — in church, in society, in the individual. He will expect Christianity to be a Centaur, — half horse, half man; a Laocoön struggling with the serpents from the sea; a seed fighting its way against frost and darkness towards the light and life. He will recur continually to his definition that evolution is a continuous progressive change by means of resident forces. He will remember that the divine life is resident in undivine humanity. He will not be surprised to find the waters of the stream disturbed; for he will reflect that the divine purity has come into a turbid stream, and that it can purify only by being itself indistinguishably combined with the impure. When he is told that modern Christianity is only a "civilized paganism," he will reply, "That is exactly what I supposed it to be; and it will continue to be a civilized paganism until the civilization has entirely eliminated the paganism." He will not be surprised to find pagan ceremonies in the ritual, pagan superstitions in the creed, pagan selfishness in the life, ignorance and superstition in the church, and even errors and partialisms in the Bible. For he will remember that the divine life, which is bringing all life into harmony with itself, is a life resident in man. He will remember that the Bible does not claim to be the absolute Word of God; that, on the contrary, it declares that the Word of God was with God and was God, and existed before the world was; that it claims to be the Word of God, *as perceived and understood by holy men of old*, the Word as spoken to men, and understood and interpreted by men, who saw it in part as we still see it, and reflected it as from a mirror in enigmas. He will remember that the Church is not yet the bride of Christ, but the plebeian daughter whom Christ is educating to be his bride. He will remember that Christianity is not the absolutely divine, but the divine in humanity, the divine force resident in man and transforming man into the likeness of the divine. Christianity is the light struggling with the darkness, life battling with death, the spiritual overcoming the animal. The end is not yet. We judge Christianity as the scientist judges the embryo, as the gardener the bud, as the teacher the pupil, — not by what it is, but by what it promises to be.

The doctrine of evolution is not inconsistent with the existence of types of arrested development, nor with deterioration and decay. The progress is continuous, but not unbroken. Nature halts. She shows specimens of unfinished work. Evolution is not all onward and upward. There are incomplete types, stereotyped and left unchanged and unchanging; there are no-movements, lateral movements, downward movements; there is inertia, death, decay. The Christian evolutionist is not therefore surprised to find all these phenomena in the evolution of Christianity. His finding them there does not shake his faith in the divine life which struggles toward victory against obstacles, and sometimes seems to suffer defeat. He expects to find faith hardened at certain epochs into cast-iron creeds; thought arrested in its development; men struggling to prevent all growth, imagining that death is life and life is death, that evolution is dangerous and that arrested development alone is safe. He expects to find pagan superstitions sometimes triumphing over Christian faith, even in church creeds; pagan ceremonies sometimes masquerading in Christian robes, even in church services; and pagan selfishness poisoning the life blood of Christian love, even in communities which think themselves wholly Christian.

"A growing tree," says Professor Le Conte, "branches and again branches in all directions, some branches going upward, some sidewise, and some downward, — anywhere, everywhere, for light and air; but the whole tree grows ever taller in its higher branches, larger in the circumference of its outstretching arms, and more diversified in structure. Even so the tree of life, by the law of differentiation, branches and rebranches continually in all directions, — some branches going upward to higher planes (progress); some pushing horizontally, neither rising nor sinking, but only going further from the generalized origin (specialization); some going downward (degeneration), — anywhere, everywhere, for an unoccupied place in the economy of Nature; but the whole tree grows ever higher in its highest parts, grander in its proportions, and more complexly diversified in its structure." Consciously or unconsciously, Professor Le Conte has borrowed his figure from Christ. The mustard seed is growing to be the greatest of all herbs; but it grows in all directions; some branches pushing upward to higher planes; some growing only further and further away from the original stock, different therefrom in apparent direction, yet the same in nature and in fruit; some growing downward and earthward; some with fresh wood and fresh leaves; some halting in their growth and standing stunted and dwarfed, yet living; some dead, and only waiting the sharp pruning knife of the gardener, or nature's slower knife of decay; yet the whole "higher in its highest parts, grander in its proportions, and more complexly diversified in its structure" than when the Nazarene cast the seed into the ground by the shores of Gennesaret. Then, a solitary physician, healing a few score of lame and halt and blind and lepers by a touch or a word, — now, throughout all lands which his presence has made holy, hospitals for every form of disease known among mankind; then, a single feeding of five thousand men, beside women and children, seated in serried ranks upon the ground, — now, an organized benefaction, which, through the consecrated channels of commerce, so distributes to the needs of man, that in a truly Christian community a famine is well-nigh impossible; then, a single teacher speaking to a single congregation on the hillside and illustrating the simplest principles of the moral life, — now, unnumbered followers, so instructing men concerning God, duty, love, life, that not only does every nation hear the truth in a dialect which it can understand, but every temperament also in a language of intellect and emotion unconsciously adapted to its special need.

Does any Christian think that such a view is lacking in reverence for the Master? He may settle the question with the Master himself, who said, "Greater works than these shall ye do; because I go to my Father."

I may perhaps assume that the scientist, if he accepts religion in any sense, will not object to this view of Christianity. If he believes that man is a spiritual being and possesses a spiritual life, he will welcome the attempt to trace the development of this life according to the now generally accepted principles of evolution. But certain religious minds will at once interpose an objection. The religious life will seem to them to be an exception to the general law of evolution. They may hesitate to formulate an objection which their feeling really interposes. They may even be startled if they attempt to formulate such an objection, by discovering that, in so doing, they are denying the unity of life, and thus in fact, though not in form, throwing doubt upon the unity of God. But they will easily find this objection formulated for them. They will find it stated by Lord Macaulay in the interest of rationalism. "All divine truth," he says, "is, according to the doctrine of all Protestant churches, revealed in certain books. It is equally open to all who, in any age, can read those books; nor can all the discoveries of all the philosophies of the world add a single verse to any of those books. It is plain, therefore, that in divinity there cannot be a progress analogous to that which is constantly taking place in pharmacy, geology, and navigation. A Christian of the fifth century with a Bible is neither better nor worse situated than a Christian of the nineteenth century with a Bible, candor and natural acuteness being of course supposed equal."[1] They will find the same objection to progress in religion stated with equal vigor by Dean Burgon, but in the interest of theological conservatism. "The essential difference between theology and every other science which can be named is this: that whereas the others are progressive, theology does not admit of progress, and that for the reason already assigned, viz., because it came to man, in the first instance, not as a partial discovery, but as a complete revelation. Whereas, therefore, in the investigation of natural phenomena, man's business is to discover something *new*, theology bids its professors inquire for what is *old*."[2]

This objection cannot be met by analogical arguments from other departments of thought and life, for its gist lies in a supposed contrast between theology, the science of the divine life, and all other sciences. The Bible is interpreted, alike by Lord Macaulay and by Dean Burgon, alike by the apostle of a cultivated agnosticism and by the representative of a conservative ecclesiasticism, as a bar to progress in theology. It would be vain to point out that the Christian-

[1] Macaulay's Essay on Ranke's "History of the Popes," *Miscellaneous Works*, vol. ii. p. 618.

[2] Dean Burgon, in the *Fortnightly Review* for April, 1887, p. 606.

ity of the nineteenth century is not the same as the Christianity of the first century. The reply will be that it is not the same because of the decadence into which the church has fallen. We turn, then, to the Bible itself, since those who deny that progress may be predicated of religion claim to base this denial wholly upon the Bible, and ask whether it claims to prevent or to promote progress in religious thought ; whether its command is "halt" or "forward march;" whether, in Dean Burgon's phrase, it forbids men to discover aught that is new, and commands those who believe in it to inquire only for what is old.

To ask this question is to answer it. The most casual glance at the Bible discloses the fact that, from its opening to its closing utterance, it is the record of progress, a call to progress, an inspiration to progress. Its face is always set towards the future. The story of the Fall in Genesis is in some respects similar to that in other ancient legends; but Genesis alone contains a promise of restoration, "He shall bruise thy heel, but thou shalt bruise his head." Poisoned shalt thou be by the spirit of evil, but the spirit of evil shall be ground to powder beneath thy feet at last. The story of the Deluge is common to Genesis and other traditions as ancient or more ancient; but it is in Genesis that the rainbow spans the retreating cloud, bidding man look forward with hope to a divinely ordered future. Abraham is led out of the land of his idolatry by a promise to be fulfilled, not in his time, but in that of his children's children. Israel is summoned out of Egypt by the expectation of a future prosperity for which the past and the present give no warrant. The Tabernacle in the Wilderness is a preparation for a Temple in the Holy Land. The Temple is destroyed forever, and with it the idolatrous idea that God's presence is confined to holy places, or his revelation of himself to particular forms; in its place, seventy years of exile give to the Jewish people the Synagogue and the Holy Scriptures. From Genesis to Malachi the faces of patriarch, prophet, and priest are turned to the future: the religion of the Old Testament is a religion of expectancy; the hope and faith of Israel are fixed upon a Coming One. The condition of the Jews is exactly the reverse of that which Dean Burgon recommends; their theology makes it their business to look for something new, not to inquire for and be content with what is old.

Three or four centuries pass by. The new dispensation opens with a prophecy and a promise. Its first word turns all thoughts to the future. Prepare ye the way of the coming Lord is the burden of John the Baptist's message. Jesus takes up the cry. His preaching is also a summons to hope and expectancy: "The kingdom of God is at hand." The people dwell in their past; he summons them continually to the future. They are content with Moses and the prophets; he not only proclaims another and a better law, but he also declares in unmistakable terms his relation to the old: it is unfinished, he comes to complete; it is undeveloped, he comes to ripen. The process will be gradual; the consummation requires time. His kingdom is not a completed kingdom: it is a seed cast in the ground; it is a wheat-field growing up for a future harvest. His teaching is new wine, it requires new bottles; it is a new life, it requires a new garment. The institutions of Christianity must be elastic, because Christianity itself is a growing religion, with a life greater in the future than in the present. As the end draws near, Christ gathers with his disciples outside the walls of Jerusalem, and as the setting sun gilds the spires and domes of the Holy City, he foretells the destruction of Jerusalem, and bids his disciples take a long look forward, through the gloom of that dreadful day, to a redemption to be perfected and a Second Coming of the Redeemer. He meets them in the upper chamber, where he repeats the message in tenderer words:

he has many things to say to them which now
they are not able to bear; they must wait for the
best; it lies in the future.   As he ascends out
of their sight, the angelic word to them is that
they must look for his reappearing, and through
patience, hope, and a blessed activity prepare for
it.   That which inspires the apostles, as they take
up their work, is not the memory of a great
past, but the hope of a great future.   They are
as those that seek a country.   They are pil-
grims and strangers, and their haven lies before
them.   They forget the things that are behind;
they press forward for their prize.   They count
not themselves to have attained; they follow
after, if they may apprehend that for which they
are apprehended in Christ Jesus.   They look
for a new heaven and a new earth in which
dwelleth righteousness.   They exhort one another to grow in grace and in knowledge.   And
when at last the canon closes, the last vision
which greets our eyes is not a completed city,
but a city still descending out of heaven upon
the earth; not a completed victory, but a Captain riding forth conquering and to conquer;
not a kingdom accomplished, but an hour yet to
come when the kingdoms of this earth shall have
become the kingdom of our Lord and of his
Christ.   From the vague promises of redemption in the first chapter of Genesis to the clear

vision of victory in the last chapter of Revelation, the cry of patriarch, prophet, martyr, apostle, and seer is the cry of the Lord to Moses by the shore of the Red Sea: "Speak unto the children of Israel that they go forward." If Lord Macaulay and Dean Burgon are right, if "theology does not admit of progress," Moses could not have added to Abraham's call the clearer words of the Ten Commandments, nor David supplanted the Tabernacle with preparations for a Temple, nor the prophets of exile have encouraged the organization of the synagogues, nor the Master substituted the Sermon on the Mount for the Mosaic Law, nor Paul have completed the wisdom of Proverbs and Ecclesiastes with the diviner and profounder wisdom of the Epistles to the Romans and to the Ephesians.

This whole notion of revealed religion consisting in a revelation made once for all and therefore forbidding progress, or confining it within very narrow limits, — to the criticism and interpretation, for example, of a Book or a restatement of what the Book says, but in slightly different forms of speech, — grows out of a singular misapprehension of the nature of revelation. The sun in the heavens is obscured by the clouds; through a break in the clouds it appears for an instant; the navigator catches its place, makes up his record, and by that record thenceforth steers his vessel. So the ancient prophets are conceived to have caught a glimpse of divine truth, entered it in their log, and given us the reckoning by which ever after the world is to be navigated. But this notion of revelation, as something external to man, is as inconsistent with Scripture as it is with the analogies of all education and the fundamental principles of psychology. Revelation is unveiling; but the veil is over the mind of the pupil, not over the face of the truth. This veil is removed and can only be removed gradually, as the mind itself acquires a capacity to perceive and receive truth before incomprehensible. The figure is not original with me; I borrow it from Paul: "Even unto this day when Moses is read, the veil is upon their heart. Nevertheless, when one shall turn to the Lord, the veil shall be taken away." The heavens are not veiled from the pupil, but the pupil is veiled, so that he cannot comprehend the stellar spaces, magnitudes, movements, until education has removed the veil and so revealed the truth.

As in physical, so in moral science, revealing is a psychological process. It is the creation of capacity, — moral and intellectual, or both. In the nature of the case it can be nothing else. Truth cannot be revealed to incapacity. That

God is love is the simplest, as it is the most fundamental revelation concerning God which his Word contains. But it means and can mean no more than love means to the individual soul. The child in the infant class prattles it artlessly, scarcely knowing the meaning of the word. The maiden sees a new and deeper meaning in it, as love looks out of her eyes into the eyes of the bridegroom at the altar. The mother has a new revelation when the babe upon her bosom strikes a new note of love in her heart. The aged saint, through the joy and the sorrow of love, the hunger and the satisfaction of love, love at the marriage, love in the home, love at the open grave, has learned something more, though not all, of the height and depth, the length and breadth of love immeasurable; the text lightly dropped from her lips in childhood she cannot speak without bowed head and tearful eyes. As with the individual, so with the race: love means in the Nineteenth Century what it could not mean in the First; from the lips of a Henry Ward Beecher what it could not mean from the lips of an Augustine or a Calvin.

Thus the Bible is not so much a revelation as a means of revelation. It is a revelation, because beyond all other books it stimulates the moral and spiritual nature, stirs men to think and feel, awakens their life, and so develops in them a capacity to perceive and receive the truths of the moral and the spiritual order. God is not veiled, but man is blind; and the Bible opens the eyes of the blind. The church has indeed often adopted, consciously or unconsciously, the philosophy of Lord Macaulay and Dean Burgon; it has endeavored to crystallize truth into a formal and final state. For a creed is truth crystallized. But a crystal is a dead thing, and truth is living. Truth is not a crystal, it is a seed. It is to be planted, and what comes from the planting will depend as much on the soil in which it is planted as on the seed itself. The figure is Christ's. "A sower went forth to sow; some seed fell by the wayside, some upon stony places; some among thorns; some into good ground and brought forth fruit, some an hundred fold, some sixty fold, some thirty fold." Which way does the seed look: backward to the winter or forward to the autumn? The fundamental difficulty about all attempts to define truth in a creed is that truth is infinite, and therefore transcends all definitions. As soon as humanity understands the creed, the creed ceases to be to humanity the whole truth; because there is truth yet beyond, not confined within the creed. The fundamental difficulty in all attempts to reduce truth to a dogma is that they are attempts to reveal truth without imparting life. But truth cannot be revealed except as life is imparted; for we can know only as we live. Revelation is, of psychological necessity, progressive; for we know the truth only as we grow in life-capacity to know the truth. The Bible never falls into the error of the church. It never attempts to reduce truth to a dogma, never crystallizes it in a creed. The value of the Bible is not that it furnishes men with thought, but that it makes them think. The Bible is a revelation because it is a literature of power; it operates on humanity for cataract; it removes the veil from the readers' eyes; it stirs them to see truth with their own eyes and to think it in their own thoughts.

In fact, this has always been the effect of the Bible. Churches, creeds, and theological and ecclesiastical systems have often repressed thought, checked it, or at least tethered it. The Bible has emancipated the mind, set men thinking, and created differences and divisions. Not without historical warrant does Kaulbach, in his cartoon of the Reformation, group all the intellectual activity of the Seventeenth Century around Luther with his open Bible in his hand. The Bible reveals truth not by making it so plain that men need not study, but by making it so fascinating that they must study. Lessing said that if one offered him Truth in the one hand and Search for Truth in the other, he would choose Search for Truth. Search for Truth the Bible has given to man ever since the Waldenses studied it in secret in their mountain fastnesses, and by it fed that independence and individuality which the ecclesiasticism of their age had almost extirpated everywhere else in Europe.

The belief, then, that the Christian religion is a divine life is not inconsistent with the belief that it is an evolution, since evolution offers no explanation of the nature or origin of life; it only explains life's process. The belief that the Bible is a revelation from God is not inconsistent with the belief that the Christian religion is an evolution; for revelation is not a final statement of truth, crystallized into dogma, but a gradual and progressive unveiling of the mind that it may see truth clearly and receive it vitally. The Bible is not fossilized truth in an amber Book; it is a seed which vitalizes the soil into which it is cast; a window through which the light of dawning day enters the quickened mind; a voice commanding humanity to look forward and to go forward; a prophet who bids men seek their golden age in the future, not in the past.

CHAPTER II.

THE EVOLUTION OF THE BIBLE.

ACCORDING to Max Müller, religion consists in "the perception of the Infinite under such manifestations as are able to influence the moral character of man." According to Professor Le Conte, evolution is "continuous progressive change, according to certain laws, and by means of resident forces." According to the evolutionary theory, therefore, revelation will be such a manifestation of the Infinite as is able to influence the moral character of man, made, however, not perfect and complete at the outset, but in a series of continuous progressive changes, according to certain laws, and by means of a spiritual force or forces in the men who are themselves the media of this revelation. The current questions in Christian circles respecting the Bible may all be reduced to the question whether revelation is thus a progressive revelation, with those incompletenesses and imperfections which are necessary accompaniments of progression, or whether it is a complete and perfect revelation, unchanging and unchangeable from the outset, and like its divine Author, the same yesterday, to-day, and forever.

The question, therefore, to which I invite the reader's attention in this chapter is not whether the Bible is an inspired literature and contains a divine revelation. To deny this is to deny Christianity. He who disbelieves in the Bible as the text-book of 'revealed religion is not in his belief a Christian, whatever he may be in his character. He is, properly speaking, a theist. The Bible has a unique place in the literature of the world. It has comforted the sorrowing, inspired the apathetic, guided the perplexed, strengthened the weak, and called to practical repentance the sinful and the erring. No theology can be true which takes this Bible out of human life, weakens its sacred authority, makes it less valuable as an inspiration and a guide, reduces it to the commonplaces of the world's thought, and degrades it and deprives it of its life-giving power. There is no better test of spiritual truth than spiritual fruitfulness; and in making our estimate of truth and falsehood we must take into account the spiritual as well as the logical faculties, the testimony of the intuitions as well as the conclusions of the judgment.

But, on the other hand, the question is not whether this Bible has in it some incidental inaccuracies and imperfections: whether some of its dates are wrong, some of its words and phrases mistranslated, miscopied, or even originally mischosen; whether there are differences in detail in its parallel narratives, showing an absence of absolute and minute accuracy; whether there are, as a conservative theologian has conceived that there are, some specks of sandstone in the marble. The question is far more fundamental. How are we to regard the Bible? How are we to regard inspiration and revelation? Are we to think that God has given us a perfect and infallible standard, something complete and perfect from its inception; or are we to think that he has given us a literature in which the manifestations of his presence and power are unique, but in which they are made through men of like passions as we ourselves are, men who saw truth as in a glass darkly, men who knew in part and prophesied in part? Is the Bible like the Northern Lights, flashing instantly and without premonition upon a world of darkness, and setting all the heavens aglow with its resplendent fire; or is it like the sunrise, silvering first the mountain tops, gradually creeping down the valleys, a progressive light, mingled with, yet gradually vanquishing the darkness, its pathway like that of the righteous man, growing brighter and brighter unto the perfect day?

The first of these opinions has been very gen-

erally held in the churches born of the Reformation. The Reformers repudiated an infallible church, and, when asked what authority
they would substitute therefor, replied, "The
Bible." They did not indeed at first claim for
the Bible, as we have it to-day, absolute iner-
rancy. Luther almost contemptuously repudiated the Epistle of James as an epistle of straw.[1]
But as the battle between the Roman Catholic
and the Protestant churches went on, the Protestant theologians, for polemical reasons, laid
more and more stress on the authority of Scripture, and the doctrine of infallible inspiration
crept into the church. With it came the general claim for the Bible that it is an absolute
and an infallible authority upon all subjects, —
science, chronology, history, literature, rhetoric,
theology. The revelation was regarded, more or
less consistently, as a complete and perfect revelation given to Moses at the outset. Pagan
beliefs and institutions parallel to those of the
Mosaic dispensation were supposed to have been
borrowed from Biblical revelation. The incon-
sistency between the practices of Israel and this
earlier revelation was regarded as degeneracy and
apostasy, incidents of the Fall. The object of
the prophets was supposed to be to reform and

[1] See, for further illustration, Hagenbach's *History of Christian Doctrine*, sec. 243, note 1.

restore the original revelation. And the New Testament was interpreted, not as an addition and enlargement to the spiritual knowledge of the world, but only as a revelation in a new form of the truth which the world had received in the Garden of Eden.

No one any longer really believes this; but a great many attempt to believe it, or to make themselves believe that they believe it. Thus fragments of this belief still remain in an incongruous no-system of theology, fragments which it is well-nigh impossible to put together in a connected and coherent whole. As a system it cannot be described, but the fragments which remain of it, found in different systems, may be sketched by way of illustration.

The man, then, who holds, or thinks he holds, or desires to hold this conception of the Bible, as a complete, perfect, and flawless revelation of divine truth from the beginning, finds in its first chapter a history of the creation which he regards as a divine revelation of the mode of the world's formation. This chapter declares that the world was made in six days by successive utterances of God, and that the writer may leave no doubt as to his meaning, he declares that evening and morning made each successive day. But our devout reader, who has begun by believing the Bible to be an authority on natural sci-

ence, abandons the earlier belief that the world
was made by divine utterances in six days, because all geological science establishes the contrary beyond peradventure. First, he conceives
that day means an epoch, and cites in support of
his conclusion the statement that a thousand years
are with the Lord as one day; then he supposes
with Hugh Miller that the revelation was not
according to reality, but according to appearance, that the process of creation was seen in
a vision by the inspired prophet ; and finally
he modifies his original theory respecting the
supreme authority of the Bible by concluding
that it is not an authority in matters of natural
science. He reads the story of man's creation
and believes that he is infallibly taught that man
was made out of the dust by a sculptor's process,
six thousand years ago. Anthropology demonstrates to him that man has been upon the earth
a considerably longer time than this, and he
concludes, after ruminating upon this fact, that
the Biblical chronology was introduced into the
Bible in the time of Archbishop Usher, in the
sixteenth century, and is not a part of its infallible revelation. He reads the story of the Fall,
with its tree, the fruit of which was to make man
immortal, with its weedless garden, and its talking serpent, and its death following sin. He
learns again from science that death has existed

in the world from the beginning, and must have existed, that the immortality of man's body is an impossible conception, and that all science more and more tends to the conclusion that man as an animal has been developed by gradual processes from a lower animal condition. As in defending his conception of a revelation perfect and complete from the beginning he first fought geology as irreligious, and then the antiquity of man as irreligious, so now he is fighting the doctrine of evolution as irreligious, not knowing to what new position he can retreat if his belief in the historical verity of the Fall is taken from him.

He reads on in his Bible, and finds that the political laws of this book gave allowance to, if not direct approval of, polygamy and slavery. If he be a Mormon, he avails himself of its authority and pronounces polygamy a patriarchal institution; if he be a slave-holder, he pronounces slavery to be a patriarchal institution; but if he be neither, he concedes that these laws, giving an apparent sanction to lust and covetousness, are not divine ideals, but a concession to the infirmity of human flesh. In support of this position he cites Christ, but he fails to see that he has already conceded that the revelation is not the perfect and flawless manifestation of a divine ideal which at first he thought it to be.

It is quite possible that he passes by the ecclesiastical laws altogether, but if he studies them he does not comply with them. The early revelation required circumcision; but his children are not circumcised. It required worship to be performed only in the Temple, or chiefly there, but he rightly believes one place to be as sacred as another. It forbade all conduct of public worship except by the children of a single specified parentage, but in his church the conduct of public worship is thrown open to any man properly equipped, spiritually and intellectually, for the performance of that function. It provided as a form of worship a system of sacrifices; the bleating of sheep and the lowing of cattle mingled in the Temple with the chants of praise, and rivers of blood flowed underground from the sanctuary; but in his church there are neither cattle, sheep, nor doves. And yet he thinks, or thinks that he thinks, that originally this ecclesiastical cult was framed in heaven and given to man, and he endeavors to preserve, or imagines that he endeavors to preserve, some traces of it in his own worship. Baptism has taken the place of circumcision; in his prayers, though nowhere else, he calls his meeting-house a temple; perhaps he calls his minister a priest, or, if Protestant prejudices do not permit this, he confers upon him quasi priestly functions, which grow less and

less, until at last the only clerical act which a
layman may not perform is to pronounce a bene-
diction, — as though a prayer for the blessing of
the Father, the Son, and the Holy Spirit on a congregation could be asked only by an ordained
clergyman. His communion table he calls an
altar; possibly he even preserves in the service
thereat, in the unbloody sacrifice of the Mass, an
attenuated form of the Jewish sacrificial system;
or, banishing it from worship altogether, still
clings to it tenaciously by insisting that in the
creed the word sacrificial shall be coupled with
the atonement. The evolutionist recognizes a
spiritual continuity between the past and the
present, and in the earlier forms a primitive expression of that life of God in the soul of man
which survives all changes of ritual; but in spite
of specious arguments, any man of common
sense, putting side by side the Jewish ritual and
the Puritan forms of worship, instantly perceives
that the modern service is by no means conformed
to the earlier one as to a complete, perfect, authoritative, and final revelation.

Perhaps this student finally concludes that,
as the Bible is not a final authority in science, so
the Mosaic law is not a final authority in ecclesiasticism. Perhaps, though he can find no authority for it whatever in either Christ or Paul, he
assumes that the New Testament has abolished

the ceremonial law, not one jot or tittle of which Christ declared should pass away until all be fulfilled. He makes his stand upon the declaration that the moral laws of the Old Testament constitute the final and authoritative word of God upon the subject of the moral life. But even to those moral laws he pays no literal obedience. Unless he is a Seventh Day Christian, he works on the seventh day with the rest of his neighbors, and takes another day in the week for his rest and his religious observances. In the chancel of his church, by the side of the law, "Thou shalt not make unto thee any graven image," he puts without hesitation the bas-relief of the last pastor. He finds himself involved by his theory in moral perplexities from which he endeavors in vain to escape. He reads the story miscalled the Sacrifice of Isaac, and no argument can make it seem to him really possible that God, who has implanted in every father's heart the command to protect his child, uttered to one father the command to kill his child. He reads in some imprecatory Psalm the prayer of the Psalmist that God will not forgive Israel's enemies; he reads the Sermon on the Mount, with its command from the Master to love our enemies, and pray for those that injure us; and no exegetical skill can make the two morally harmonious. How can the first be a complete and perfect transcription of the divine will, since the second flatly contradicts it?

There is danger in skepticism, but there is greater danger in shams; in making-believe believe; in trying to think something which is not really thinkable, or at least is not really thought; in shutting our ears and our hearts to the truth which is knocking for admission. The Master never condemned honest doubt, but shams of all sorts were odious to him. He denounced the Pharisees who for a pretense made long prayers; he put out of the room the hired mourners who simulated grief; and the dissimulating Judas Iscariot he bade depart, before he would commence his last sacred conference with his disciples. He who was the Truth could not endure a lie. Let us be true with ourselves, come what may to our theology.

An infallible book is an impossible conception, and to-day no one really believes that our present Bible is such a book. Theologians maintain, indeed, that the original utterances of the original writers were infallibly accurate, but we have not the original utterances of the original writers. An infallible book is a book which without any error whatever conveys truth from one mind to another mind. In order that the Bible should be infallible, the original writers must have been infallibly informed as to the truth; they must have been able to express it infallibly; they must have had a language which was an infallible vehicle for the communication of their thoughts; after their death their manuscripts must have been infallibly preserved and infallibly copied; when translation became necessary, the translators must have been able to give an infallible translation; and finally, the men who receive the book must be able infallibly to apprehend what was thus infallibly understood by the writers, infallibly communicated by them, infallibly preserved, infallibly copied, and infallibly translated. Nothing less than this combination would give us to-day an infallible Bible; and no one believes that this infallible combination exists. Whether the original writers infallibly understood the truth, or not, they had no infallible vehicle of communicating it: their manuscripts were not infallibly preserved or copied or translated; and the sectarian differences which exist to-day afford an absolute demonstration that we are not able infallibly to understand their meaning.

God has not given us an infallible standard, but something far better, namely, a divine revelation. There is one relatively infallible book in the world, — Euclid's Geometry. It was written years before Christ, and, so far as I know, no material errors have been found in it from that day to this; but it has exerted no such influence upon mankind as the Bible. It is inerrant, but it is not divine. The value of the Bible consists not in the supposed fact that there are no errors in it, but in this, that its books have been written by men who, with various degrees of clearness of vision, saw God in his world of nature and in his world of men, and were able to make others see him. It is God — God's truth, God's life — revealed in and imparted by the Bible which makes it a sacred book; and that impartation is all the better, and that revelation is all the clearer, because men were the media through which the life was imparted and the revelation was made, — men who saw the truth, as we see it, in a glass darkly, and who knew it, as we know it, in part only.

As a collection of literature, the Bible is unquestionably the result of evolution. It is a library of sixty-six different books, written by between fifty and sixty different writers. If we assume, as I think we may, that the first writings of the canon [1] date from the age of Moses and the last from the close of the first century, this

[1] I do not say books. Into the vexed question of the age of the Pentateuch I do not enter. But I do not doubt that it contains writings — the Ten Commandments, for example, and in my judgment much more — which date from the days of Moses.

volume is the product of about sixteen centuries of national life. During these centuries, the religious teachers of Israel, the men who had in themselves that life of God which is the essence of religion, who perceived in themselves and in life such a manifestation of the Infinite as produced a real change in their moral nature, instructed the people concerning this life, occasionally by writing, generally by speech. Parts of what they spoke were by others reduced to writing; parts of what were thus reduced to writing were preserved; parts of what were thus preserved were incorporated in what is known as the Bible. This incorporation in a single volume was not effected at a definite date [1] nor by any well-defined authority. The process by which the books, both of the Old Testament and of the New Testament, were selected was a gradual one. The canon of the Old Testament, substantially as we now possess it, existed at the time of the translation of the Hebrew into the Septuagint, about the third century before Christ. But even to-day the Christian church is divided upon the question what constitutes that canon, Roman Catholic theologians, and some

---

[1] " For the opinion, often met with in modern books, that the canon of the Old Testament was closed by Ezra or in Ezra's time, there is no foundation in antiquity whatever." — Canon Driver, *Introduction to the Old Testament*, p. xxxi.

Protestant theologians, placing as high a value on the apocryphal books as on some of the so-called canonical books.

The New Testament grew in a similar manner. At first the infant church depended on oral reports for a knowledge of the sayings and the acts of Christ. These were in time reduced to writing by different biographers. The apostles from time to time wrote letters of counsel to the different churches. These biographies and these letters were interchanged. Gradually the larger churches acquired a collection of these fragmentary writings. The first approximation to a canonical collection of these books dates from the second century of the Christian era, but it does not include all the books in the present canon, which did not assume its present form till the close of the fourth century; nor is it possible to state exactly when or by whom the various books were first collected and formally recognized as one collection. Thus, both the Old Testament and the New Testament were constructed by a process of natural selection. As collections of literature both can be described, in terms of an evolutionary philosophy, as the result of a practical process of selection and elimination, or as "a struggle for existence and a survival of the fittest."

As the collection of books which constitutes

the Bible was formed by a gradual process, so a gradual development is to be seen in the teaching contained in the collection. The later books present higher ideals of character and conduct, clearer and nobler conceptions of God, more catholic and more positive interpretations of his redeeming work in the world, than the earlier books. The revelation is a progressive revelation. The forms, whether of religious thought, of public worship, or of church order and organization, in the Bible are not the same; those of the later ages have grown out of those of the former ages, and are superior to them. In brief, the Bible is the history of the development of the life of God in the life of a peculiar people; and it traces the development of that life from lower to higher and from simpler to more complex forms. It is the record of a spiritual evolution; of a clearer and ever clearer perception of the Infinite, under such manifestations as tend to produce a continually higher and stronger moral influence on the character and conduct of men. We can most easily trace this process of evolution by considering the Bible in four aspects, as a volume of history, of laws, of ethics, and of theology.

1. The book of Genesis is a collection of narratives of prehistoric events. No one supposes that all of it was written by contemporaneous

authors. Adam is not credited with the authorship of the chapter about Eden, nor Noah with the story of the Deluge, nor Abraham with the record of the first great migration. The unknown author or editor of Genesis does not tell us how he obtained his knowledge of these events. He does not claim that the facts were revealed to him; and no later Biblical writer makes this claim for him. The natural presumption therefore is that he obtained his information, as most writers obtain their information concerning events outside their own observation, by investigation, inquiry, and collation of preëxisting material. Luke tells us how he obtained his knowledge of the facts which make up his biography of Christ: he obtained them from others, who were eye-witnesses and ministers of the word. Presumptively, the writer of Genesis obtained his knowledge in a similar way, and this presumption is greatly strengthened by two circumstances. In the first place, a careful analysis of the book makes it clear that it is composed of two or more narratives which have been put together by an editor. The book of Genesis is a Harmony analogous to the Harmonies of the Gospel, which have been composed at various times by piecing together in a continuous narrative the Four Gospels. In the second place, narratives of the Creation, the Temptation and

Fall, and the Deluge, in important respects analogous to those in Genesis, are found in early
traditions, some of them apparently older than
even the most remote date assigned to Genesis
by any scholar. The Hebrew prophet's account
is unique, not because of the events narrated,
but because of the spirit in which he has narrated them. He has taken the material as he
found it, and with that material has re-written
the early history of the world, and written God
into it.

"The first chapters of Genesis," says Lenormant, "constitute a 'Book of the Beginnings,'
in accordance with the stories handed down in
Israel from generation to generation, ever since
the times of the Patriarchs, which in all its
essential affirmations is parallel with the statements of the sacred books from the banks of the
Euphrates and Tigris. But, if this is so, I shall
perhaps be asked, Where then do you find the
divine inspiration of the writers who made this
archæology, that supernatural help by which, as
a Christian, you must believe them to have been
guided? Where? In the absolutely new spirit
which animates their narration, even though the
form of it may have remained in almost every
respect the same as among the neighboring nations. It is the same narrative, and in it the
same episodes succeed one another in like man-

ner; and yet one would be blind not to perceive that the signification has become altogether different. The exuberant polytheism which encumbers these stories among the Chaldæans has been carefully eliminated, to give place to the severest monotheism. What formerly expressed naturalistic conceptions of a singular grossness, here becomes the garb of moral truths of the most exalted and most purely spiritual order. The essential features of the form of the tradition have been preserved, and yet between the Bible and the sacred books of Chaldæa there is all the distance of one of the most tremendous revolutions which have ever been effected in human beliefs. Herein consists the miracle, and it is none the less amazing for being transposed. Others may seek to explain this by the simple, natural progress of the conscience of humanity; for myself, I do not hesitate to find in it the effect of a supernatural intervention of divine Providence, and I bow before the God who inspired the Law and the Prophets." [1]

The Christian evolutionist, with Lenormant, does not suppose that the facts narrated in the book of Genesis were supernaturally revealed to the historian. He finds for the writer no such claim anywhere in the Bible; and he sees no rea-

[1] *Beginnings of History*, by Francis Lenormant. Charles Scribner's Sons. Preface, pp. xvi, xvii.

son to make such a claim in the writer's behalf.
He supposes that a devout soul, who had in himself the power of spiritual perception, and who
saw God in his world, set himself to write the
beginnings of history in such a way that those
who were familiar with these prehistoric legends
should hereafter see God to have been with the
race from the beginning. He indicates this purpose in the opening sentences of his narrative:
"In the beginning God created the heavens and
the earth." The material universe, which the
pagan nations deified and worshiped, he perceives to be the creation of a divine mind, and
he so represents it. That depersonification of
nature which Greek philosophy did not accom-
plish till centuries later confronts us in the opening chapter of Genesis. Other religions taught
man to fear natural phenomena as gods. This
unknown prophet teaches that God made the
world and all it contains, for man's habitation
and use, and made man to exercise a divine control over it. That God is the Creator of the
world, that man is God's child, and is made in
God's likeness, that sin is disobedience to God,
that penalty is separation from God and loss of
the life of God, that God began redemption on
the day in which man began to sin, — these are
the lessons of the first chapter of Genesis: and
they are equally valuable whether one believes or

disbelieves that the description of creation in the first chapter of Genesis is scientifically accurate, or the account of the Garden of Eden in the third chapter of Genesis, with its miraculous life-giving fruit and its talking serpent, is historically accurate. The lessons which the divinely inspired prophet found in life and wrote into the already current history of a prehistoric age are alike inspired, whether the scientific and historical materials were revelations or traditions.

This perception of God in history characterizes all the historic records of the Old Testament. Abraham leaves the land of his nativity that he may find God and may worship him. Joseph illustrates faith in God alike in the dungeon and in the palace. God proves himself in the plagues of Egypt above all the gods, and calls his people out of bondage that they may become the people of God. God fights for them and with them; their victories are his victories, and their land the land which he has given them. And in all the subsequent history, from the colonial days through the days of imperial splendor, later division and degradation, and final exile and captivity, we have not the annals of a great nation, not the glorification of great leaders and the memorial of splendid achievements, but history written by men who saw God in history, and wrote that they might enable us also to see him, as a God of righteousness. It is all written to elucidate the principle that "righteousness exalteth a nation, but sin is a reproach to any people." In this is the divineness of the Bible history: not in the accuracy of its chronological and historical details, but in its perception of the spiritual meaning of life's great drama. That meaning is not really less in the history of the United States than in that of Palestine; but the Hebrew historians perceived that meaning, and so told the story that all readers perceive it. This constitutes the essential difference between the Hebrew Scriptures and the modern press. In the Hebrew Bible is a perception of the Infinite manifesting himself in the national life; in the American newspaper, for the most part, only a perception of party policies, politicians, strifes, defeats, and victories.

2. As Biblical history traces the development of the divine life in the nation, so Biblical laws exemplify the development of that life. The Levitical law is not a revealed code of worship to be literally obeyed by the Jews and symbolically obeyed by other peoples. Circumcision, temple, priesthood, altar, sacrifices, did not originate with Moses, and were not confined to the Jewish people. The great lawgiver finds these forms of the religious life in the surrounding

nations. He accepts them, gives them a new
meaning, and adapts them to a higher and better
life. A movable tent will serve as well for worship as a splendid Temple; for wherever we
gather to meet God in reverence and holy desire,
there he is. The nation must have a priesthood,
for to abolish it at this epoch in human history
would be to abolish all religious service and all
that feeds and fosters the religious life; but the
priesthood are deprived of that power which in
all lands and all ages has made it dangerous.
The priests have no share in the ownership of
the land; and are made wholly dependent upon
the voluntary offerings of the people, — voluntary, I say, for though the amount to be contributed is definitely determined, there is no
process provided for enforcing it as a tax. The
priestly claim to be the sole teachers of the people is repudiated, and the teaching function is
throughout Israel's history left to be exercised
mainly by a wholly unorganized and unofficial
body of prophets. Altars are prohibited; one
only may be built; and this of the simplest construction. "An altar of earth shalt thou make
unto me; . . . and if thou wilt make me an
altar of stone, thou shalt not build it of hewn
stone." Sacrifices are allowed; but the spirit
which in pagan lands sacrificed prisoners, and
offered hundreds of cattle and sheep is exorcised.

Human sacrifice is forbidden; sacrifices are never measured by their magnitude or value. A single bullock, or a lamb, or a pigeon, or even a sheaf of wheat, — anything will do, so that it be not some defective thing, of no use for other purposes, and so that it be offered in simplicity and sincerity. Any lawyer, subjecting the Levitical statutes to a lawyer's examination, would not hesitate to declare that they are regulative, not mandatory, that is, that their object is not to require altar, and sacrifice, and priesthood, but to regulate, restrain, and limit these ecclesiastical institutions already existing.[1] In the history of Israel there is the same controversy between ecclesiasticism and spirituality, high church and low church, ceremonialism and simplicity, which has characterized the church in all ages. A striking illustration is afforded by the 51st Psalm, in which the original prophet declares that "the sacrifices of God are a broken spirit," and a later priestly writer adds, with curious incongruity, "Build thou the walls of Jerusalem; then shalt thou be pleased with burnt offering and whole burnt offering." It is an addition quite in the spirit of much modern

---

[1] My authority for this statement is my brother, Austin Abbott, Dean of the New York University Law School. It is abundantly borne out by a careful and unprejudiced study of the laws.

hymn tinkering. Mediæval European history is, in this respect, almost an exact reproduction of mediæval Jewish history. The priests are always urging the importance of Temple and altar and sacrifice; the prophets are always insisting that these are valuable only as the instruments of a devout spirit, and that to obey is better than sacrifice. At last, with the coming of Christ, the whole system of sacrifice comes to an end. The sinners come to him, and he habitually bids them go in peace and sin no more. Only once does he send men to the Temple, and then as a sanitary measure, that the cure of their leprosy may be officially ascertained and pronounced. Not once does he bid a penitent to offer any sacrifice for his sins.

The Christian evolutionist, then, does not see in the Levitical code a divine authority for a sacrificial system to be maintained in attenuated forms, as in a bloodless sacrifice of the Mass, or a perpetuated phrase in a creed. On the contrary, he takes account of the notion universally prevailing among pagan peoples, and not yet eliminated from Christian lands, that God must be appeased by pain and approached by sacrifice; he sees in the Levitical code a permission of sacrifices, because their abolition could not have been comprehended by a primitive and spiritually uneducated people; but he also sees that

these sacrifices are not so much commanded, or
commended, as restrained, limited, and dimin-
ished; he sees prophet after prophet declaring,
either that they are utterly valueless, or valuable
only as the expression of religious feeling and
purpose; he sees Christ, even when in close
proximity to the Temple, disregarding the sacrificial system altogether in his treatment of repentant sinners; he sees Paul declaring that we
need no other sacrifice and no other mercy-seat
than Christ. He believes that the sacrificial
system represents a profound spiritual truth,
the truth that it costs to forgive sin; of this
truth I shall have something to say in a subsequent chapter. He recognizes in the ceremonial law of the Old Testament, not a law to be
universally obeyed, either literally or symbolically, by all peoples, but part of a system of
education, a "continuous progressive change,"
from that conception of God which regards him
as an offended King, to be approached only in
fear, with an offering and by a court ceremonialism, to that conception of God which regards
him as a Father, to be approached with the un-
ceremonious confidence· of unfrightened childhood.

The Christian evolutionist looks upon the
political laws of the Jews in the same way.
There are three great organic sins destructive

of any society which harbors them: war, which is destructive of national order, and while it lasts turns the nation into an armed camp; slavery, which degrades labor and forbids the education of the laborers, that is, of the vast majority of the population; and polygamy, which makes family life impossible, and in the individual substitutes lust for love. These three organic sins are inevitably characteristic of the earlier and more barbaric states of society: for combativeness, which is the inspiration of war; idleness, which is the inspiration of slavery; and lust, which is the inspiration of polygamy, are the three animal vices which are fastened upon man as he first issues from an animal condition. The evolutionist sees these facts clearly; but being an evolutionist he has more faith in education than in law, in growth than in manufacture, in other words, in resident forces working from within than in external forces operating from without. He does not think that it is the function of government to enforce moral ideals upon an uneducated community by penal enactment. He sees therefore in the political law of the Jews the same evolution which he sees in their ecclesiastical law.

A prophetic lawgiver perceives that war is not an honorable avocation for a nation, and issues laws in restraint of war; he perceives that slavery cannot enrich a people, and issues laws in restraint of slavery; he perceives that polygamy cannot promote welfare, and as a consequence issues laws in protection of womanhood. The evolutionist thinks no better, but rather worse, of slavery and polygamy because they are "patriarchal institutions;" and he measures the Mosaic laws on the subject by their effect, which already in the time of Christ had been such as practically to abolish both the harem and the slave from loyal Jewish households, and has now made the Jewish people, whatever other faults they may possess, the most industrious and the most chaste people on the face of the globe.

3. As the ecclesiastical and the political laws, so the moral laws of the Bible afford no perfect ideal of life at the outset, but show a "continuous and progressive change" from a simple to a more complex, from a lower to a higher law. There are certain fundamental principles which underlie all social order, the habitual violation of which can end in nothing but anarchy. These are such as the following: reverence for a righteous God as the only real Lawgiver, so that on the one hand the state has no right to enact or enforce a law not divine in its nature, and on the other the individual must obey, not because there is force to compel him, but because conscience requires obedience; some

stated time redeemed for self-development from toil and drudgery, else man sinks back into the animal and life becomes a prison house; respect by children for parents, indispensable to home government, order, and training; respect by every man for the three great fundamental rights of his neighbor, — life, property, and family relationships.

The Ten Commandments prohibit the more palpable violation of these principles. These commandments are not only wonderful expressions of social righteousness for that early age, but the principles embodied in them underlie all our modern criminal legislation. But they are not, and are not intended to be, final moral ideals for the life of the individual. One might keep each one of these statutes, except perhaps the last, and not be admitted to good society of to-day. He might not swear, but might be vulgar and obscene. He might not commit adultery, but might be sensual, licentious, and an habitual drunkard. He might not steal, but might run a faro table or a lottery shop.

Nor is it correct to say, as it sometimes has been said, that Christ gives to these commandments a personal and spiritual interpretation, which clothes them with a different meaning. For Christ does not say, It hath been said to them of old time, Thou shalt not kill, and what they meant was, Thou shalt value life. He says, *But* I say unto you, Be not angry without a cause. He puts his law in sharp contrast with the ancient law. There is as little reason for saying that Christ re-affirms and spiritualizes the Ten Commandments, as there is for saying that he re-affirms and spiritualizes the law, An eye for an eye, and a tooth for a tooth.

The Ten Commandments are simply prohibitions of the more palpable violations of the laws of social well-being. They do not afford, and are not intended to afford, God's ideal of moral character or conduct. Later in Jewish history a higher ideal is presented; in such utterances as, "Thou shalt love the Lord thy God with all thy heart and soul and strength;" "Thou shalt love thy neighbor as thyself;" "Who shall ascend unto the hill of the Lord, and who shall stand in his Holy Place? He that hath clean hands and a pure heart." Yet these are not the Christian ideal. When Christ is asked, Which is the great command of the Law? and replies, "Thou shalt love the Lord thy God with all thy heart and soul and strength, and thy neighbor as thyself," he does not in his answer give his ideal of life. He simply repeats the Jewish ideal, as it is expressed in two general laws found in the Jewish books. To love one's neighbor as one's self is not the Christian law of love;

it is the Jewish law of justice. Who am I, that I should expect better treatment than or higher regard from my neighbor than I accord to him? Christ's ideal is quite different. He gives it to his own disciples, in his last interview with them before his death. "A new commandment give I unto you," he says; "that ye love one another as I have loved you." Did he love his disciples only as he loved himself? He that beggared himself that he might make us rich, he that emptied himself of divinity that he might make us divine, he that lived and loved and suffered and died for those that were unworthy of his sacrifice, loved us far more than he loved himself. This ideal of love he left as a legacy for his followers; and it is not an impossible one for us. Paul loved the Gentile world better than himself; and every true missionary has done so. William of Orange loved his country better than himself; and every true patriot has done so. William Lloyd Garrison loved the enslaved better than he loved himself; and every true reformer has done so. The true mother loves her child better than herself; the nurse her patient; the martyr his church. It is not the Ten Commandments which should be put up in our churches, as the ideals of our moral life for us to pattern after. They are but the primitive prohibitions of the grosser sins against social order. In their place should be put the New Commandment, "That ye love one another as I have loved you."

This conception of moral evolution in the Bible reconciles incongruities and relieves difficulties, which on the theory of a perfect and complete revelation at the outset are morally and intellectually unendurable. That God should tell a father to kill his child, it is impossible really to believe. He would be commanding by special edict what by a law written in the universal conscience he has prohibited. A few years ago a father sincerely believed that he had received such a command; and the community unanimously adjudged him to be insane. But that in those early ages a devout father should know that he must consecrate his child, even his only begotten child, to God, and in his ignorance should imagine sacrifice by death to be the only possible form of such consecration, and that God should interpose to teach him, and through him his descendants, that life, not death, is the true consecration, — that it is not difficult to believe. That God should command the children of Israel to exterminate the Canaanites, slaying men, women, and children, the same God whose patient love was manifested in the life and character of Jesus Christ, it is impossible to believe. But it is quite possible to believe that in a primitive age a people should be inspired with an enthusiasm for righteousness by their prophets, and with a wholly sacred determination to destroy, root and branch, the iniquities which made the Canaanites the most corrupt nation of a corrupt age; and that they should be unable to see any other way of destroying the sin than by destroying the sinners, having no even remote conception of the possibility of converting and educating them.   Even in the Christian church in the nineteenth century, there is a very general unbelief in the efficacy of any measures for the conversion of pagan peoples to a higher and purer life.   It is impossible to believe that God, who through his Son bids his children "Love your enemies; do good to them who despitefully use you, and persecute you, that ye may be the children of your father which is in heaven," should have inspired a persecuted Hebrew in exile to execrate Babylon with the words, "O daughter of Babylon, who art to be destroyed; happy shall he be that rewardeth thee as thou hast served us; happy shall he be that taketh and dasheth thy little ones against the stones." But it is not impossible to believe that a Hebrew, in this hour of utter bitterness, experiencing the cruel scorn of a people who derisively demanded of their captives an exhibition of their sacred psalmody, — somewhat as we sometimes call upon the North American Indians to amuse us with their war songs and their war dances, — in the very frankness of his soul should have breathed out to God the bitterness of a wholly unchristian hate, and in so doing should have found relief. It is not the unknown author of the imprecatory Psalms who says "Follow me;" it is Christ; and the imprecatory Psalms remain to show us out of what bitterness of feeling he delivers those that follow him. To go back from the Sermon on the Mount to the imprecatory Psalms, and try to find a divine ideal in them, is as if Bunyan's Pilgrim should go back from the Land of Beulah to the Slough of Despond, because he began his pilgrimage by floundering therein.

4. The object of the Bible is primarily, not a revelation of law, either ecclesiastical, political, or moral, but a revelation of God. This revelation is both imperfect and progressive. It is imperfect, because it is the revelation of the infinite to the finite, and the finite cannot perfectly comprehend the infinite; it is progressive, because as man grows in spiritual and intellectual capacity, his apprehension of the infinite grows also. This proposition is as familiar to the student of theology as it is axiomatic. "If," says Professor Harris, "God reveals himself, it must be *through the medium of the finite*, and to

finite beings. The revelation must be commensurate with the medium through which it is made and with the development of the minds to whom it is made. Hence, both the *revelation* itself, and man's apprehension of the God revealed, must be progressive, and at any point of time *incomplete*. Hence, while it is the true God who reveals himself, man's apprehension of God at different stages of his own development may be not only incomplete, but marred by gross misconception."

The Bible illustrates this truth. The revelation of God grows both in clearness and in spiritual grandeur as man grows in capacity to receive and to communicate it. Moses' conception of God is superior to that of Abraham, David's is superior to that of Moses, Isaiah's is superior to that of David, and Paul's is superior to that of Isaiah.

The conception of creation bodied forth in the first chapter of Genesis is very different from that found in the Chaldean tablets or the Phœnician mythology; but the difference is religious, not scientific; that is, it is a difference, not chiefly in the nature of the phenomena recorded, but in the spirit in which they are recorded and in the perception of the One whose nature they manifest and whose glory they express. In the more ancient Chaldean tablets, chaos forms the gods; in Genesis, God out of chaos forms the world. In the Chaldean accounts of the creation of men, Belus "commanded one of the gods to cut off his head and mix the blood which flowed forth with earth, and form men therewith, and beasts that could bear the light. So man was made and was intelligent, being a, partaker of the divine wisdom."[1] In Genesis, God forms man out of the dust of the earth and breathes into him the breath of the divine life. In brief, to quote Lenormant, the prehistoric narrative in Genesis is the same as in the Chaldean tablets; "in it the same episodes succeed one another in the same manner; and yet one would be blind not to perceive that the signification has become altogether different. The exuberant polytheism which encumbers these stories among the Chaldeans has been carefully eliminated to give place to the reverent monotheism." Thus the progressive revelation begins with the conception of God as the creator of the world, and of man as made in the image of God; therefore of God as spirit, and of matter as the creature of and subordinate to spirit. Yet this monotheism is by no means always clear at first. Generally God is represented as the one and only true God; sometimes, however, as only a

[1] Lenormant's *Beginnings of History*, p. 491. Rawlinson's *Ancient Monarchies*, vol. i. p. 143.

God above all other gods. And while the former
is certainly the view generally entertained and
pressed upon the people by the prophets, the second is the view generally entertained among the
people. It does not seem absurd to them to
think that they cannot conquer the Philistines in
the plains because their God is not the God of
the plains; nor to imagine that golden calves,
representing the sacred bulls of Egypt, may
serve to symbolize the gods that brought them
up out of Egypt. It is at least a fair question
whether the plural form Elohim (gods) used by
one of the writers of Genesis is not an indication
that the prevailing polytheism of the pagan nations had not in these earliest times entirely dis-
appeared from the minds of even the inspired
prophets.

The monotheistic conception lays the foundation for the next step in the progress of the revelation of God to his people: this, namely, that
God is a righteous God. The first distinct
statement of this truth, to us so fundamental
and even axiomatic, is in the narrative of Abraham's interview with God, and in this interview
it is not asserted dogmatically, not assumed as
axiomatic, but put in a tone of expostulation and
entreaty: "Shall not the Judge of all the earth
do right?" This conception of God as a God
that is righteous and does right is brought clearly

into prominence in the revelation to and through Moses. Even more than monotheism does this distinguish the religion of the Hebrews from that of the pagan nations. Out of this grows naturally and necessarily the conception of religion as righteousness. Unorthodox writers see this as clearly as the most orthodox. "The conditions of Jahveh's covenant with his people," says Renan,[1] "are exclusively moral; he recompenses them with prosperity in this world, giving it to those who please him, and the man who pleases him must be irreproachable. In order to enjoy a long life and to be happy, a man must avoid evil. The great step is taken. The old religions, in which the god granted his blessings to those who offered him the first sacrifices and who most carefully observed the ritual of his worship, were quite left behind."

Life often seems inconsistent with this faith in a righteous God who rewards righteousness and punishes sin. For often the righteous suffer and the wicked prosper. Out of this terrible tragedy of life, this incongruity between life and the moral sense of man assuring him of the divine nature of righteousness, the drama of Job is constructed. Only as it gradually dawns upon the spiritual vision that this is not all of life, and that another life may bring compensation and

---

[1] *History of the People of Israel,* ii. 336.

adjust the unequal balances, does faith in the righteousness of God reassure itself. At first the most spiritual prophet cannot conceive that a righteous God should forgive sin. Overlook it he cannot; and the cure of it by patient love is at first not seen at all, and later only dimly, imperfectly, and gradually. Joshua, indeed, distinctly tells the people that they cannot serve Jehovah because he will not forgive their sin; and Moses sometimes implies the same, sometimes the reverse. Moreover, at first Jehovah is the God of the nation rather than the God of the individual. He is the God of Battles, the God of the Host of Israel, a Man of War, a Captain, a King; he marches at the head of the nation, directs its campaigns, gives it the victory. In the earlier history he is rarely referred to by terms which indicate personal filial relations between the soul and himself, as a Shepherd, a Father, a Friend. The phraseology of religion is that of the camp rather than that of the household. But by David's time this new and tenderer and deeper conception of God has begun to dawn on the mind of Israel. Repeatedly by the Psalmist is Jehovah addressed as "*my* God," a phrase apparently used but twice before David's time. In the Hebrew Psalter, God is seen to be a merciful God, a personal Friend redeeming even more than judging the world.

"Who forgiveth all thine iniquities;
Who healeth all thy diseases ;
Who redeemeth thy life from destruction ;

. . . .

The Lord is full of compassion and gracious,
Slow to anger, and plenteous in mercy.
He will not always chide ;
Neither will he keep his anger for ever.
He hath not dealt with us after our sins,
Nor rewarded us after our iniquities.
For as the heaven is high above the earth,
So great is his mercy toward them that fear him.
As far as the east is from the west,
So far hath he removed our transgressions from us."

Nothing like this, scarcely anything approximating this, is to be found in the Pentateuch. The only even partial parallels are in Deuteronomy, which there is at least good reason to believe was written towards the close of the monarchy. But even in the Psalms God is still the God of Israel; and still in the main the ground of appeal to him is the righteousness of him who appeals. It is not till Isaiah, the Second Isaiah,[1] that God is clearly revealed as a God whose mercy, as well as justice, extends to all the inhabitants of the earth. Israel is still the chosen people of God, but chosen to be a light to lighten the Gentiles. God is still a just God,

[1] Nearly all modern critics regard Isa. xl.–lxvi. as written a century later than the preceding portion of the book, and by another author, designated as the Great Unknown, or sometimes as the Second Isaiah.

but a God whose justice is mercy, and whose righteousness redeems. And a glimpse, the first in this resplendent progress of man's acquaintance with God, is given of that divine suffering love which is at once to judge and to redeem the world, in the person of the Suffering Servant of Jehovah, who bears the iniquities of Jehovah's people, and by his justice justifies many.

Thus the Christian evolutionist sees in the Bible not a complete and perfect revelation of science, history, law, ethics, or even theology; he sees man gradually receiving God's revelation of himself. The Bible is not an infallible standard of truth or life. It is the history of the growth of man's consciousness of God. It is the expression of God in human thought, God speaking to man and through man, God speaking through the selected writings of the selected prophets of a selected people. Thus it is truly *a* standard; but not a final and infallible standard. Its history is composed, as other histories have been composed, out of such materials as were at hand or could be secured; but the historian saw, what other contemporaneous historians did not see, God in his world, and wrote the history with God manifested in it. The laws, ceremonial and political, do not afford, and are not intended to afford, a final form for either worship or justice;

they are suited to their times, and are such forms as are best adapted to express worship and to execute justice in a rude age and among a barbarous people; and they are the more divine because they are not perfect, but are with divine compassion adapted to an early age and fitted to prepare for better days to come. The earliest moral laws are not ideals for the individual conduct and character; they embody such regulations as are necessary to social order, like the regulations in a school, without which order, and therefore intelligent progress, would be impossible; and they express such ideals as could be apprehended by man in the earlier stages of his moral development. Their value consists, not in the fact that they afford a moral standard for all time, but in the fact that they prepare men for a better standard in the future. And the earliest conceptions of God, while immeasurably superior to those embodied in the pagan literature about, and superior to many that even now prevail in intelligent circles in the United States, are inferior to those which are expressed in the experience of the later prophets. Each successive age sees God more-clearly and interprets him more clearly than does its predecessor, until the fullness of time has come, and the Word no longer speaks through the broken utterances of men, but becomes incarnate.

CHAPTER III.

THE EVOLUTION OF THEOLOGY.

The Old Theology.

THE Bible is a book of religion, not a book of theology. The questions which the Hebrew mind asked were questions of religion, not of theology. Let us recur to Max Müller's definition of religion: "Religion consists in the perception of the Infinite under such manifestations as are able to influence the moral character of man." The Hebrew prophets, then, sought for such a perception of the Infinite as would influence the moral character of those to whom they spoke. They did not ask the question, What is God? but, What is the way to Him? Nor, What is the nature of sin? but, How shall we get rid of it? Nor, What is the origin of pain? but, How shall we make a true spiritual use of it? The Bible accordingly contains few or no definitions. None of God, unless "God is love" be regarded as a definition; none of sin, unless "Sin is lawlessness" be regarded as a definition; none of faith, unless "Faith is the substance of things hoped for, the evidence of things not seen," be regarded as a definition; and absolutely none of atonement, regeneration, the forgiveness of sin, the nature of Christ, or the divine attributes.

The book of Job, if not in authorship the oldest in the Bible, undoubtedly represents the earliest religious life. It is a picture of Hebraic thought in its beginnings. If not written before the Mosaic law, it is written to portray a prior state of society. There is in it no reference to the Mosaic dispensation, to the sacrifices, to the Ten Commandments, or to any explicit revelation. It is a book of questionings, rather than of answers. Job is a theist, living before revelation. He has believed that God is a righteous God, and will reward righteousness and punish iniquity. He has been righteous, and yet he has suffered overwhelming disaster. When his friends insist that he must have sinned, otherwise this disaster would not have come upon him, he repudiates indignantly their explanation. He is too honest to pretend a confession which is not real. His utterances are the cry of a perplexed soul. He interprets the problem of life as it presents itself, not to the philosopher in his study, but to men and women in the actual experiences of their life. "Oh, that I knew where I might find him," he cries, "that

I might come even unto his dwelling place. I would set in order my cause before him." Unable to find God, he longs for some mediator who shall interpret him. "He is not a man as I am, that I should answer him, and we should come together in judgment. Neither is there any Daysman [*i. e.* mediator or umpire] betwixt us that might lay his hand upon us both." He longs for some clear revelation that will interpret to him the enigma of his own personal life, and will make clear to him what he should do. "Oh that I had the indictment which mine adversary had written; surely I would carry it upon my shoulder, I would bind it unto me as a crown." These are not the questions of philosophy, but of life. They are evoked out of spiritual struggle; they are far profounder, more serious, more agonizing, than the questions which the philosopher calmly ponders in his study, surrounded by his volumes.

To these questions the Hebrew prophets afforded, even in the Old Testament, partial answers. They did not attempt to define God, but they did point the way to him.

" Who shall ascend into the hill of the Lord ?
Or who shall stand in his holy place ?
He that hath clean hands, and a pure heart ;
Who hath not lifted up his soul unto vanity, nor sworn deceit-
    fully.

He shall receive the blessing from the Lord,
And righteousness from the God of his salvation."

These prophets did not attempt to define the nature of sin, but they did point out the remedy.

"Wash you; make you clean; put away the evil of your doings from before mine eyes; cease to do evil; learn to do well; seek judgment; relieve the oppressed; judge the fatherless; plead for the widow. Come now, and let us reason together, saith the Lord: though your sins be as scarlet, they shall be as white as snow; though they be red like crimson, they shall be as wool."

The prophets did not discuss the origin of pain. They did not puzzle themselves over the problem how, into a world governed by love, sin and suffering have come. They sought for peace in an experience of trust transcending knowledge.

" Commit thy way unto the Lord ;
Trust also in him ; and he shall bring it to pass.
And he shall bring forth thy righteousness as the light,
And thy judgment as the noonday.
Rest in the Lord, and wait patiently for him :
Fret not thyself because of him who prospereth in his way."

To these practical questions of life, to which the Hebrew prophets gave partial and tentative answers, Jesus Christ gave answers fuller and more complete. He fulfilled the law and the prophets, that is, he filled out the outline sketch which they had made. He began his ministry

by proclaiming that the Kingdom of God was at
hand; then, in private conference with his disciples, he told them that he was the long-prom-
ised Messiah, come to bring that kingdom upon
the earth; and finally, he assured them that it
was through him that they were to come to God.
"I have manifested the Father's name," he said
to them. "He that hath seen me hath seen the
Father." He said nothing against the Jewish
system of sacrifices; but he absolutely ignored
it. When men came to him repentant, with the
burden of their sin, he simply told them their
sins were forgiven, and they were to arise and
go their way and sin no more; but he never
sent a penitent to the priest to offer a sin-offer-
ing for his sins. More by his deeds than by
his words he taught men that pain was not evil;
that sanctified by love it was beneficent; that it
was a glorious thing to suffer for love's sake;
that such love-suffering was to be coveted, not
fled from; and he bade his disciples take up the
cross and follow him. Thus he answered the
three great questions of religion: How to find
God; how to get rid of sin; how to utilize suffering. But his silence was only less significant
than his speech. Like the prophets who pre-
ceded him, he preached religion, not theology.
That is, he answered the vital questions of experience, not the curious inquiries of the intellect.

He furnished no catalogue of divine attributes and no definition of the Infinite, but he told men the way to God. He did not discuss the nature of sin, nor its origin, nor in one single instance the relation of the individual to the race, to his ancestry, or to Adam. But he assured men that by breaking off their sins in righteousness they might find forgiveness and relief. He never discussed the question how pain entered into the world, but he gave to pain a new meaning and to the souls of men a new inspiration, which made them eager to enter into it. Nowhere outside the church of Christ can one find such an expression as that of Paul, "I count all things but loss for the excellency of the knowledge of Christ Jesus my Lord. . . . That I may know him, and the power of his resurrection, and the fellowship of his sufferings, being made conformable unto his death."

In order to introduce Christianity into the Greek and Roman world, it was as necessary that it should be re-cast into Greek and Roman thought moulds as that it should be expressed in Greek and Roman language. For this re-casting of it, the world is chiefly indebted to the Apostle Paul. Humanly speaking, Christianity would have been only a reformed Judaism, but for him. He did not add to Christianity, as some have imagined, nor did he corrupt it, as others have imagined; neither did he simply re-iterate what Jesus Christ had taught in the forms in which Jesus Christ taught it. He translated Christianity from Hebrew into Greek and Roman forms of thought. He was the necessary link between the Hebraic and the Gentile world.

Paul seems to me to have been greatly misunderstood, alike by his admirers and his critics. He was not primarily a philosopher, loving the truth for its own sake and constructing it in carefully articulated systems. He had and expressed a vigorous contempt for mere wisdom. In his writings there are few or no references to the philosophical systems of his time. He was not by nature a logician; he did not reach his conclusions by labored processes of argument. He was a Hebrew of the Hebrews, belonging by race and by his inherent religious spirit to a people who have given the world a David and an Isaiah. He was the last of the Hebrew prophets, a seer rather than a logician. His mind was more nearly of the type of Emerson or Goethe than of the type of Calvin or Thomas Aquinas. His life was not that of a philosopher, but that of an evangelist. He traveled from city to city, preaching the gospel. The churches which sprang up where he preached, he carried as a burden on his heart. He wrote to them practical letters of counsel. From these letters and from the evangelistic sermons of which we have fragmentary reports, his system of theology has to be deduced, as one might deduce a system of practical theology from the sermons of Dwight L. Moody, or George Whitefield. His logic is often defective, and it is always the logic of an advocate. He does not hesitate to use the *argumentum ad hominem.* He appeals to the preconceived notions and the established prejudices of his hearers in order to secure their assent to the truths and principles which he is inculcating. Thus, in the ninth, tenth, and eleventh chapters of Romans, he appeals to a people who believed in election, — believed that God had chosen the Jews as his peculiar people, and had passed by all the rest of mankind. Assuming the divine sovereignty, which was the fundamental postulate of all Jewish theology, Paul argues from it that God has a right to elect the heathen and pass by the Jews, if he so chooses. He is not in these chapters arguing for election and confirming a narrow view of divine grace, but he is using a doctrine of election so firmly established in his auditors' hearts as to be ineradicable, in order to give them an enlarged conception of divine grace and lead them to the final conclusion that "God hath shut them all up together in unbelief that he might have mercy upon all."

But while Paul was by nature a Hebrew and

a prophet, he lived in a scholastic age and received a scholastic education. There were no prophets in Judæa, no poets in Greece. The greatest genius is at once a product and a cause of his times. In Paul, scholasticism overlaid a spiritual nature, and at the same time scholasticism was voluntarily chosen by a spiritual nature as an instrument for the production of spiritual realities. Thus this man, evangelist and prophet in his essential nature, was philosopher and scholastic and dialectician in his forms of thought, partly because education modified his nature, partly because it was his nature to be, as he himself said, "all things to all men," if by any means he might save some.

But the problems which interested him were the Hebraic rather than the Greek problems, the problems of religion, not those of intellectual curiosity: not the question how to define God, but how to find him; not how to account for sin, but how to get rid of it; not how to explain the existence of suffering, but how to maintain a life of peace and joy in the midst of pain. That this was his purpose he has expressed again and again in the autobiographic aspirations for himself and for those to whom he ministered. His letters abound with such prayers as "That ye might be filled with all the fullness of God." "The very God of peace sanctify you wholly." "The peace of God which passeth all understanding keep your hearts and minds through Christ Jesus." These are the utterances of a man the inspiration of whose life is, not curiosity to solve difficult thought problems, but a great desire to enrich in himself and in others the spiritual life of faith and hope and love. For the accomplishment of this purpose he translated Christ's answers to the great problems of our spiritual life into Greek and Roman forms of thought. The history of Christian theology is the history of the intermixture of his answers with pagan philosophy, and of the gradual process by which the gospel, as Christ proclaimed it and Paul interpreted it, pervaded, purified, and transformed pagan conceptions.

The ancient world of thought may be divided into three classes: the Oriental or mystic, the Greek or philosophical, the Roman or legal. We shall perhaps best trace the progress of the Old Theology by considering it under these three aspects.

1. The Oriental does not think, — he meditates; the Occidental does not meditate, — he thinks. The object of the Oriental is vision, the object of the Occidental is action. To see God is the supreme religious desire of the one; to do God's will is the supreme religious desire of the other. The combination of Orientalism with

Christianity gave gnosticism. The predominating characteristic of gnosticism was its unreality. Matter had no real existence, or existence only as an emanation of pure thought. Sin and evil were not, they only seemed to be. The spiritual was the only actual; all else was as the phantasmagoria of a dream. God was the only reality. God is good, therefore nothing but goodness really exists. Individualism is separation from God, and therefore evil. The end of religion is not life, that is, individuality, but absorption in God, that is, ceasing to live. In various forms this Orientalism has at times reappeared in the Christian church, usually as a reaction and protest against legalism and dogmatism. It is needless here to trace its successive appearances as mysticism, pietism, quietism. In our own time a lingering survival of it is seen sometimes in spiritual experiences expressed in such a hymn as

> " Oh to be nothing, nothing,
>   Only to lie at his feet,
> A broken and empty vessel
>   For the Master's service meet."

Sometimes it appears in exotic forms of semi-religious philosophy, as in the spiritual exaltation which says, " Believe that you are righteous, and you are righteous," or even " Believe that you are well, and you are well."

Between this Oriental gnosticism and the

practical religion of the Old and New Testaments there is little in common. It is not a broken and empty vessel, but a whole and full one, which is for the Master's service meet. The life which Christ inspires leads to the prayer to be something, not nothing, and ever something more and more. The end of his religion is not absorption in God, but an individual life filled full of the spirit of God. Pain, disease, death, are not unreal evils to be imagined out of existence; they are blessed realities to be used by the spiritual soul in growing Godward. Sin and evil are not phantasmagoria, but terrible realities, and the battle against them to which we are called is the battle, not of an insane man with his dreams, but of soldiers against an actual foe. So, in spite of its occasional and episodical appearances in the Christian church, Oriental gnosticism has never gotten a foothold in Christendom; and on the other hand, Christianity, though its cradle was in the East, traveled not eastward but westward, and has never yet succeeded in pervading Oriental countries. Not its methods only, but its very principles and aims, are radically different from those of Oriental philosophy.

2. The Greek mind was speculative. The Athenians, who "spent their time in nothing else, but either to tell or to hear some new thing,"

were characteristic Greeks. The problems of Greek philosophy were not like those of the Hebrew prophets. The Hebrew asked, What shall I do? The Greek, What shall I think? So the Greeks looked to the new religion to tell them, What is God? What is sin? What is the origin of evil? At the same time Christianity brought with it new problems, to the solution of which they set themselves. Paul said that Jesus Christ had come into the world to answer the question of the Altar to the Unknown God: "Whom ye ignorantly worship, him declare I unto you." Straightway the Greek began to ask, Who is this Christ, and what is his relation to the Infinite? Paul said that Jesus Christ is the power of God unto salvation. The Greek began to ask, What kind of power? How does he effect salvation? In what consists the efficacy of his life and death? To these and kindred speculative questions the Greeks gave their strength. The result was not primarily a righteous life, but a philosophical system. The answer to speculative questions never does more than send the questioner back of the answer to ask a new question more difficult than before. The spirit of speculation was not allayed, but stimulated, by discussion, until finally the scholastic debates reached their climax in the extraordinary contradictions of the Athanasian Creed:

" Whosoever will be saved: before all things it is necessary that he hold the Catholic faith. Which faith except every one do keep whole and undefiled: without doubt he shall perish everlastingly. And the Catholic faith is this: That we worship one God in Trinity, and Trinity in Unity. Neither confounding the Persons: nor dividing the Substance (Essence). For there is one Person of the Father: another of the Son: and another of the Holy Ghost. The Father uncreate (uncreated): the Son uncreate (uncreated): and the Holy Ghost uncreate (uncreated). The Father incomprehensible (unlimited): the Son incomprehensible (unlimited): and the Holy Ghost incomprehensible (unlimited or infinite). The Father eternal: the Son eternal: and the Holy Ghost eternal. And yet they are not three eternals: but one eternal. As also there are not three incomprehensibles (infinites); nor three uncreated: but one uncreated: and one incomprehensible (infinite). So likewise the Father is Almighty: the Son Almighty: and the Holy Ghost Almighty. And yet they are not three Almighties: but one Almighty. So the Father is God: the Son is God: and the Holy Ghost is God. And yet they are not three Gods: but one God. So likewise the Father is Lord: the Son Lord: and the Holy Ghost Lord. And yet not three Lords: but one Lord."

Whether these speculative answers to the speculative questions of the Greek mind are right or wrong, intelligible or unintelligible, profoundly significant or without real significance, I do not here inquire. Whatever opinion one may entertain of the creed as the embodiment of an intellectual system, it is perfectly clear that it does not answer, and does not even pretend to answer, the Hebrew questions, How shall I find God? and How shall I become like him? Be the answers true or false, they are intellectual answers to an intellectual problem. They are not and do not pretend to be spiritual answers to a spiritual problem. The difference between the Athanasian Creed and the Twenty-fourth Psalm, or the Parable of the Prodigal Son, is not a difference in philosophy, it is a difference between speculation and religion. The very nature of duty and life is differently regarded: in the teaching of Jesus Christ, duty consists in loving the Lord your God with all your heart and soul and strength, and your neighbor as yourself; in the Athanasian Creed it consists in believing certain enigmatical declarations respecting the interrelationships of the Infinite. Isaiah tells us, whoever will be saved must cease to do evil and learn to do well. The Athanasian Creed has nothing to say about ceasing to do evil or learning to do well. He that will be saved must think in a certain prescribed form of the Trinity. The nature of life and the conditions of salvation are quite different in the two documents. Religion has given place to theology.

3. The Roman mind was practical, not speculative; but it was also legal and governmental, not spiritual or religious. As the Oriental was given to dreams and the Greek to speculative thinking, so the Roman was given to problems of law and of government. The Roman solution of those problems was as simple as it is to us unsatisfactory. There was one Emperor at the head of the Empire, absolute in his control of it, from whom issued edicts which were of binding force on all the citizens of that Empire. Loyalty to those edicts was the one virtue recognized in the Empire; disobedience to those edicts was visited by an inexorable penalty; forgiveness was a personal pardon for a personal offense, and could ordinarily only be granted upon condition of some expiation or satisfaction of the violated law; and finally, access to the Emperor was for most men only through subordinate officials and intermediaries.

Christianity entering Rome, and beginning there, its work of transformation, was in the process itself transformed. As theology in the Orient became mystical and imaginative, and

in Greece speculative and philosophical, so in
Rome it became forensic or governmental or
imperial. By the very necessity of his intellectual condition, the Roman, as the Greek, was
compelled to organize his religious philosophy
along the lines in which he had been educated,
and to which he was accustomed. He therefore
thought of God as a great imperial Cæsar, from
whom all authority proceeded; absolute, but
always righteous and always just. He conceived
of laws as edicts or statutes proceeding from this
imperial God, inexorable, certain to be administered, against which no man could throw himself without being destroyed in the collision.
He thought of the Bible as a book of statutes,
explaining and promulgating these edicts of the
imperial God to the sons of men. It was essential in his conception, therefore, that this statute book should be without any error or any
mistake. A mistake in the transcription of a
statute of the legislature of the State of New
York, if it does not absolutely vitiate the statute, vitiates it for all practical purposes. We
are to be governed by the written record of the
will of the legislature, not by the unknown will
which has been mistakenly reported. The
Roman theology, therefore, conceived of the
Bible as an absolute and inexorable record of
the laws which this imperial God had issued for

the government of his subjects. Sin was a violation of this law, and must be punished; because, if it were not punished, anarchy, disorder, and the disruption of this great divine empire would be the inevitable result. If any mercy were shown to the sinner, if he were pardoned, then something must be found that would be a substitute for this punishment, in order that justice, the character of the imperial God, and the sanctity and the greatness of law might be maintained. This God was too august and too remote to be immediately approached. Only through subalterns and intermediaries could he be reached. The Son must intercede with the Father, the Virgin Mary with the Son, the saints with the Virgin Mary, and finally the priests with the saints. Such, roughly sketched, was the system of Roman or imperial theology in its final development, as theologically organized by Augustine and ecclesiastically perfected by Hildebrand. It differed from the Greek in that it undertook to answer the practical questions, How shall I approach God? How shall I be delivered from the burden of sin? In this respect Augustinian theology was a distinct advance over Athanasian or even Nicene theology. But it borrowed the formulas of Roman government for its answers. It did not go with Christ to the family for a parable to interpret the relation of God to humanity; it went to imperial Rome. Its God was not an All-Father, but an infinite and eternal emperor. Its government was not one of redeeming love, but of imperial, inexorable justice. The Roman theology was forged in the same fires and cast in the same mould as the Roman hierarchy; and the two must eventually stand or fall together.

When the Reformation burst upon the world, all theology seemed at first to be swept away by this cyclone from the north. The Reformers were charged with being infidels and atheists. They were in some measure iconoclasts. Their movement was at first partially destructive. It was necessary to organize a new and reformed theology to take the place of the old. Then it was that John Calvin rose upon the world with his doctrine of divine sovereignty. He was the theological organizer of his epoch. His service to mankind is far more liable to be underestimated than overestimated.

There is, he said in effect, no king but one; no father but one. God alone is the universal King, the All-Father. Kings and hierarchies do but play at law-making; he is the only Lawgiver. Crowns and thrones and chairs are but toys; he is the only crowned and enthroned and sceptred One. From him all authority comes; in him all authority centres; to him

all allegiance is due; his will is the final, ultimate, absolute fact in the universe. It cannot
be questioned; and from it there is no appeal and
no escape. This is Calvinism, the doctrine of
divine sovereignty; to be read in the light of
the age, against whose dormant anarchy, awakening later in the French Revolution, it was a
solemn protest. Nor can we say even now, in
the United States of America, with its shallow
doctrine of popular sovereignty, its cry of *Vox
populi vox Dei*, its egotism of democracy, its
Dead Sea fruit of anarchism, that there is no
need to listen to and heed this protest of a
solemn voice, reaffirming the sublime doctrine
of the ancient Hebrew prophets, and itself reaffirmed by one of the least religiously minded
of modern historians." [1]

John Calvin's service to humanity can never
be forgotten. He was the prophet and forerun-

[1] " A king or a parliament enacts a law, and we imagine we
are creating some new regulation to encounter unprecedented
circumstances. The law itself which is applied to these circumstances was enacted from eternity. It has its existence
independent of us, and will enforce itself either to reward or
punish, as the attitude which we assume towards it is wise or
unwise. Our human laws are but copies, more or less imperfect, of the eternal laws so far as we can read them, and
either succeed and promote our welfare, or fail and bring con-
fusion and disaster, according as the legislator's insight has
detected the true principle, or has been distorted by ignorance or selfishness." — J. A. Froude, *Essay on Calvinism.*

ner of civil and religious liberty. He built
the bridge over which the church passed from a
theocratic imperialism to republicanism, for he
showed that republicanism also might be theocratic. Nor was the doctrine of election, which
he borrowed from Augustine and reaffirmed, the
narrow and exclusive doctrine which it has often
been thought to be. It is only in these later days
that the Christian church is beginning to believe
that "There's a wideness in God's mercy like
the wideness of the sea." It has always believed
in a doctrine of election. The Jews believed
that God had chosen them as his people and had
passed by the pagans. The Roman Catholic
church believed that he chose the baptized as his
people and passed by the unbaptized. In the
Inferno, Dante finds in the outermost circle of
hell the good and true of pagan nations who
have not received baptism. Calvin preached a
broader doctrine of election than that of either
Judaism or Romanism. God has chosen, he
said, whom he will, and whom he will he passeth
by. The ground of his choice lies not in the
accident of a race, it lies not in the chance of
a baptism, it lies in his own inscrutable will.
And he thus laid the foundation for the broader
doctrine that God has chosen the whole human
race, the doctrine of Paul that the grace of God
is as universal and inclusive as the sinfulness of
humanity.

But affirming the sovereignty of God, John Calvin denied the freedom of man. Any consistent system of philosophy must start either from the testimony of consciousness, accepting thereupon human freedom and human responsibility as final and ultimate facts, or it must start with the universality of law and the consequent absolute sovereignty of the lawgiver. Calvin's system was self-consistent. He declared that man had lost his freedom in the fall, and was free no more. Denying the freedom of man, he took away all incentive to activity, undermined the sense of personal responsibility by the sweeping universality of his indictment of the race, robbed the gospel of all power to convict the individual, and laid the foundation for that philosophy of necessarianism which denies not only the reality, but the possibility, of a religious or even an ethical life.[1] This imperial theology, as interpreted by John Calvin and his great master and predecessor, has been so admirably described by James Martineau,[2] that I need make no apology for transferring his description to my pages, instead of essaying a description of my own.

[1] A man with a criminal nature and education, under given circumstances of temptation, can no more help committing crime than he could help having a headache under certain conditions of brain and stomach. — J. Cotter Morison, *The Service of Man*, p. 289.

[2] *Types of Ethical Theory*, Intro. pp. 17, 18.

"The Augustinian theology is founded upon a sense of sin so passionate and absolute as to plunge the conscience into unrelieved shadows. It pledges itself to find traces everywhere of the lost condition of humanity, in virtue of which there is no longer any freedom for good, and a hopeless taint is mingled with the very springs of our activity. This doctrine is evidently the utterance of a deep but despairing moral aspiration: it estimates with such stern purity the demands of the divine holiness upon us, that only the first man, fresh with unspoiled powers, was capable of fulfilling them; and since he was false, the sole opportunity of voluntary holiness has been thrown away, and we must live in hopeless knowledge of obligations which we cannot discharge. Hence there has never been more than one solitary hour of real probation for the human race; during that hour there was a positive trust committed to a capable will, and the young world was under genuine moral administration; but, ever since, evil only has been possible to human volition, and good can pass no further than our dreams. It follows that, as the human game is already lost, we no longer live a probationary life, and can have no doctrine of applied ethics which shall have the slightest religious value; the moralities, considered as divine, are obsolete as Eden; and human nature, as it is, can produce no voluntary acts that are not relatively neutral, because uniformly offensive, to the sentiment of God. Its restoration must proceed from sources extraneous to the will; and unless snatched away in some fiery chariot of grace, it must gaze in vain upon the heaven that spreads its awful beauty above the earth. Thus a doctrine which begins with the highest proclamation of the divine moral law ends with practically superseding it. The history of the universe opens with an act of probation and closes with one of retribution, but through every intervening moment is destitute of moral conditions, and man, the central figure of the whole, — though a stately actor at the first, and an infinite recipient or victim at the last, — so falls through in the meanwhile between the powers that tempt and those that save him, that as an ethical agent he sinks into nonentity, and becomes the mere prize contended for by the spirits of darkness and of light. In this system the human personality, by the very intensity with which it burns at its own focus, consumes itself away; and the very attempt to idealize the severity and sanctity of the divine law does but cancel it from the actual, and banish it to the beginning and end of time. The man of to-day is no free individuality at all, but the mere meeting point of opposite forces foreign to his will; ruined by nature, rescued by God, — with no range of power, therefore none of responsibility between."

The Roman or imperial system of religious doctrine, known sometimes from its origin as Latin theology, sometimes from its two greatest representatives as Augustinian or as Calvinistic theology, sometimes from its legal character as forensic theology, passed from Geneva into England, and from England and Scotland to New England and so became the Puritan theology. It is august, but terrible; and equally worthy of the student's attention from the elements which it contained and those which it omitted. It put an end forever to the polytheism which had pervaded Europe; it depersonified nature, brought it into subjection to man, and made its phenomena no longer an object of terror but of utility; it gave a ground for and a sanctity to law, in its presentation of the divine Lawgiver; it laid a foundation for liberty by discovering a sanction for law in the universal conscience; it emphasized the reality and awfulness of sin, and the necessity of repentance and a new life. But it forgot that God is love, and knew him only as power; it made both law and revelation external to man, not a power and a vision within him; it made religion obedience to a government from without, not a new life working from

within; it made the church, and later the Bible,
an authority imposed on men, not a voice evok-
ing in the conscience a divine authority within;
and it denied the liberty of the individual will,
and so destroyed the sense of moral responsibility, paralyzed Christian activities, and fatally
failed in the great work of a Christian theology, that of promoting a missionary spirit.
The great missionary movements which characterize the latter part of the nineteenth century
originated in the Moravian and the Methodist
churches, each of them distinctively anti-Cal-
vinistic.

As the same social and intellectual forces
which created the Roman hierarchy created the
Roman theology, so the revival of intellectual
and spiritual life, which emancipated the church
from the former, is emancipating the church
from the latter. This emancipation it should be
our aim to facilitate, not to retard; but so to
direct that it shall be an evolution, not a revolution. The theology of the future ought to retain
all of the truth which was successively contributed
by Oriental, by Greek, and by Roman thought;
for in the evolution of Christian theology, each
of these three phases of thought made a valuable addition to the religious life of Christendom, — an addition which we cannot afford
to despise and cast away. Oriental thought

emphasized the transcendently important truth that spirit is more than matter, and is superior over matter, — a truth preëminently needed in this age, which lives by sight and scoffs at faith. Spiritual perception is as much to be trusted as sensual perception. We see moral truths as really as we see material substance, distinctions between right and wrong as truly as distinctions between red and yellow. Moral blindness is much more rare than color blindness. And if it be true that the world of sense is real, it is equally true that it is not the only reality. Greek thought emphasized the truth that religion is rational, that all its articles of faith are consonant with each other and with reason; and it prepared the way for the construction of a self-consistent system of religious thought, a system which in all its parts would realize the fundamental truth that there is possible such a perception of the Infinite as will naturally influence the mind and moral nature of men. It emphasized the truth of the divine immanence; that God is in his world of nature and in his world of men; and that he has manifested himself in the one unique and incomparable Man; and in all history by his Spirit speaking to and with men; that he is in the world revealing himself to the world, and by that revelation redeeming the world and making it a partaker of his nature. Roman thought emphasized the truth that God is transcendent; that he is not nature nor humanity, and, though in nature and in humanity, yet transcends both; that law is divine; that man can neither make nor unmake it, but only discover and apply it; and that sin is not a mere unripeness or immaturity, but a real and willful transgression of a real law, known and approved, though violated, by the sinner. Thus all three theologies contributed something toward the theology of the future: Orientalism, the reality of the spiritual and its corollaries; Grecism, the divine immanence and its corollaries; Romanism, the divine transcendence and its corollaries. The modern evolution of theological thought, popularly known as the New Theology, is partly a continuation of these three elements in a new and larger system of thought than either one singly, and partly a revulsion from the purely scholastic and forensic questions of Greek and Roman thought to the more practical and spiritual questions of Hebraic thought: How shall I find God? How get rid of sin? How utilize suffering?

How this New Theology has been developed out of the Old, by that incursion of Teutonic life and thought into Latin and Greek Christianity which led to the Reformation, will be the subject of consideration in the next chapter.

CHAPTER IV.

THE EVOLUTION OF THEOLOGY (CONTINUED).

The New Theology.

THE Lutheran Reformation was a North-Europe reaction against Roman imperialism, the protest of the Germanic race against ecclesiastical Cæsarism; a great intellectual and spiritual awakening, due to a new interpretation of Christianity by a people whose nature and traditions were individualistic. Its birthplace was Germany; its inspiration was Teutonic.

Almost simultaneously with the protests against the papal authority and the demand for an open Bible were the discovery of a Western continent and a quickened commerce, the invention of the printing-press and a revival and enlargement of literature, the birth of the scientific spirit and its application both to theoretical science and to the practical arts. Shakespeare and Cervantes, Gutenberg and Albert Dürer, Columbus and Copernicus, Loyola and Calvin, Xavier and Luther, were almost contemporaries. The first post-office, the first printing-press, the first telescope, the first spinning-wheel, were all nearly contemporaneous with the first open Bible and the first freedom of religious speech. These are not accidents. In history there are no accidents. The predominant principle of the Reformation, — the right of private judgment, — was more than a religious principle; certainly it had much more than a theological application. It was a revolt against authority. It threw humanity back upon its own resources. Rights are duties; and the right of private judgment laid upon mankind the duty of original investigation and inquiry. This right had first to be taught to man, who is always reluctant to take up a new right if it impose a new duty. The opportunity to exercise it had to be won in many a hard battle. It involved the wars in the Netherlands, the massacres in France, the civil wars in England. It cannot be said to be undisputed even now.

But by the beginning of the present century in all Protestant Europe, and even in most of Roman Catholic Europe, the right of man to think for himself had been established. It is still denied; it is still punished with ecclesiastical pains and penalties; but it no longer involves a hazard of life or limb. With the present century there began, therefore, a new era of intellectual activity, an era of individual and independent thinking. Authority was discarded; not religious authority only, but all authority over intellectual processes. The mind may be fettered, or it may be free, but it cannot long be partly fettered and partly free. Freedom is indivisible; and the right to think in either science, politics, or religion carried with it necessarily the right to think in each of the other departments of thought. Liberty to investigate led to investigation. The Baconian philosophy was a natural and necessary production of the Lutheran Reformation; and a new science of life was the natural and necessary production of the Baconian philosophy. A fresh investigation was made into history. Records that had been unquestioned were subject to scrutiny. Niebuhr gave the world a new comprehension, not merely of Roman events, but of all ancient history. Stories that had passed current for generations were subjected to a free, not to say an irreverent scrutiny. William Tell was declared to be a myth. Literature fared no better. Homer was abolished, and the Homeric ballads were attributed to an impersonal epoch. Shakespeare was reduced from the rank of a poet to that of an actor, and his plays were variously attributed to Bacon and to anonymous authors. Scientific theories which tradition had stamped as current coin in the intellectual realm were cast into the melting-pot for a new assay. Some radical errors were discovered; and each discovery made easier the work of the critic. Every hypothesis was subjected to suspicion. The whole body of scientific tradition was swept away by the same spirit which refused to own allegiance to ecclesiastical tradition. The scientific Talmuds were put away on the shelf as antique curiosities; and the world began an independent and direct investigation of phenomena, sometimes incited thereto by a spirit of iconoclastic egotism wholly unscientific, but in the main inspired by a noble curiosity, an appetite for the truth. Harvey's discovery of the circulation of the blood led to a new physiology; a new botany, a new astronomy, and a new biology followed. In the material sciences the text-books of ten years ago are already out of date.

The students of psychology were the last to catch the new spirit of the age; but they were not and could not be impervious to it. Plato was for a while closed, though we are beginning to open him again; and the scholars, turning aside from a study of what other scholars had said about man, began to study man himself. Gall, Spurzheim, and Combe discovered the intimate relations of mind and brain, and developed a science of organology which, if it is somewhat crude and has sometimes been diverted to purposes of traveling charlatans, yet represents a profound truth which science is tardily beginning to recognize. Sir William Hamilton set an example of direct study of consciousness which modern psychology is carrying forward with valuable results. It would have been strange indeed if the reaction against the despotic authority of tradition had not produced some unhealthy contempt for it, and this doubtless was the case; but we are getting beyond this first stage of the new era, and the sober-minded thinkers in all departments agree in condemning nihilism as no better in science or religion than in politics, and in commending the aphorism of Mr. Gladstone, "No greater calamity can happen to a people than to break utterly with its past."

It would have been equally strange if the impulse to original investigation and independent judgment which was derived from the religious life had not in turn affected religious thought; if, having learned in the school of conscience the right and duty of private judgment, mankind had made no attempt to exercise it in measuring the truth and value of all religious tradition; if, renouncing the authority of the ancient church, it had bowed submissively to the authority of the more modern one; if, in disowning the supremacy of the creeds of the past, it had not also disowned the supremacy of creeds fresh from the press; nay, if in its reaction, the same spirit of somewhat iconoclastic skepticism, which had repudiated Homer, should not also show itself in discussions respecting the Hebrew Scriptures. It was in the nature of things impossible that there should be a New Science, a New Politics, and a New Philosophy, and not also a New Theology. The one is no more to be dreaded than the other; and the philosophic mind will be equally unready in each instance to rush to the conclusion that the new is wholly true or wholly false.

At all events, as matter of historic fact, the same spirit of independent thought which set men to original investigation of the phenomena of vegetable, animal, social, and political life moved another class of thinkers to an independent investigation of the sources of religious truth and life; and as Protestants regarded the Bible as one of these original sources, if not the chief source, the beginning of the present century witnessed in all Protestant Christendom the beginning of an original, systematic, and enthusiastic study of the Bible. It had been studied before, but never with the same spirit manifested in the same degree. It was now for the first time a study of independent investigation. Biblical criticism assumed a new significance and a new importance. The question of the authorship and composition of the books of the Bible, the object of the writers, the circumstances under which they wrote, the audiences to which they spoke, have been studied anew and with valuable results. The libraries of Europe and even the monasteries of the East have been ransacked for manuscripts, and the manuscripts themselves have been collated and compared with an enthusiasm and a painstaking far greater than that bestowed on any secular writers of equal antiquity. The writings have been subjected to a minute and even a microscopic critical examination, and a more comprehensive study of their general tenor has not been neglected. In the theological seminaries, at first in Germany, then in our own country, a new department of "Biblical Theology" has been established, and the departments of Biblical Exegesis and Biblical Theology are coming to hold a place equal with, if not superior to, that of Systematic Theology, which had before dominated every seminary. New translations of the Scriptures have sprung up in every land; and these have proved themselves in England and America forerunners of a new revision of the English version, undertaken by representatives of the entire Protestant church. Its scholarly qualities are indubitable, whatever objections to it may be

made by a conservative spirit or a literary taste.
A new class of commentators on the Scriptures
has arisen, and a new class of commentaries
has superseded their more polemical and less
independent predecessors. Meyer in Germany,
Godet in France, and Alford in England may
not be abler as thinkers than Augustine or
Calvin; but their spirit is radically different.
They attempt neither to interpret Scripture in
harmony with a preconceived theological system,
nor even to deduce a theological system from
Scripture — hardly to prove that it is self-consistent and harmonious. They simply endeavor
to show the reader what the language of the
sacred writers, properly interpreted, means, and
leave him to deduce his own system.[1] Finally,
the whole Protestant church in Europe and
America agreed upon a course of study of the
Bible in the Sabbath-schools, in a series of pre-
arranged lessons; and so wide is the interest in
this course of Bible study that every religious
newspaper, and some secular papers, print every
week a commentary on the current lesson. These
helps are naturally not always very scholarly,

---

[1] A striking illustration of this is offered by Dean Alford's
frank declaration that there is no authority in the New Testament for the doctrine of apostolic succession. With this contrast Calvin's constant thrust at the papacy in his *Commentaries*, which are as polemically Protestant as are his *Institutes*.

the study in the Sabbath-school is not always
very thorough, and the selection of the lessons
themselves is not above criticism; but the fact
that several millions of children are simultaneously engaged in a weekly study of the Bible,
and that this Bible study has very generally
usurped the place allotted a hundred years ago,
or even less, to the catechism, is significant of
the movement of the century away from traditional authority towards independent investigation in theology, as in all other sciences. More
important than all is the concentrated attention
which this study of the church has directed towards the life and character of Christ. One has
only to compare Fleetwood's "Life of Christ"
with any one of those which are to be found to-
day upon any minister's book-shelves to perceive
the difference in the theological spirit of the
eighteenth and the nineteenth centuries. The
past half-century has produced above a score
of Lives of Christ.[1] Without concord of action they have appeared almost simultaneously
in Germany, France, Holland, England, and
America. They have been written by Jews,
Rationalists, Liberal Christians, and strict Calvinists; they represent every attitude of mind
— the coldly critical in Strauss, the rationalistic

[1] I count on my own shelves twenty-five separate Lives of
Christ; and of course my collection is far from complete.

but reverent in Hooykaas, the dramatic and imaginative in Renan, the critically orthodox in Lange and Ebrard, the historical and scholarly in Geikie and Edersheim, the devout and popular in Beecher, Hanna, and Farrar. It thus appears, from a merely cursory survey of the history of religious thought since the beginning of the present century, that the entire church has been engaged, to an extent never known before, and in a spirit never possible before, in a study of the Bible, and especially of the life of Christ. This study has been pursued by every school of thought and by every type of mind: by the rationalist and the orthodox, the critical and the devotional, the textual and the theological, the gray-haired professor and the infant-class. And all of every age and every school have been engaged, though doubtless in different degrees both of independence and earnestness, in an original investigation of the source of Christian truth and life, and with a purpose to ascertain for themselves, and from the original sources, what are Christian truth and Christian life, as interpreted by Christ and his immediate disciples.

Now it is impossible that such a study could have been pursued for over half a century and not give us something new in both theology and ethics. It is impossible that such an intellectual activity should exist and not produce some new and profound convictions, some new and clear apprehensions, and some new and crude notions which further study pursued in the same spirit will eventually correct. If half a century of study of the Bible — if, especially, half a century of study of the life and teachings of Jesus of Nazareth — did nothing to give the Christian student a clearer vision, a wider horizon, and a larger faith, hope, and charity, we might well begin to doubt whether either the Bible was the book, or Christ the person, we had thought; whether they were not correct who tell us that the world has outgrown the teaching of the one and the example of the other. If I have read aright the signs of the times, what is called the New Theology is not, properly speaking, a theology at all; it is certainly not a New England notion nor a German importation. It is the spirit of original investigation, characteristic of the age, applied to the elucidation of the problems of religious thought and life; it is a desire for a clearer understanding of the Christianity of Jesus Christ, and a quest for it in the original sources of information.

This new life led to certain sporadic protests against the Roman or forensic or Puritan theology, but these movements were both partial and local. The church of the New Jerusalem,

popularly known from its founder as Sweden-
borgianism, reintroduced into Christian theology
some of the best elements of Orientalism: reëm-
phasized the reality of the spiritual life; gave a
more spiritual conception to heaven and hell;
demanded that the Bible be read as a spiritual
revelation, not as a book of external laws; and
was emphatic in its declaration that character is
salvation, and that there is and can be no other.
In a different form the same aspect of truth
was received and emphasized by the Friends or
Quakers. Methodism, born of the earlier Mo-
ravianism, studying life from the point of view
of human consciousness, accepted its testimony
to human freedom, and by affirming what Calvin
had denied, that man *can* repent and turn to
God, gave a new and vital sense of sin, furnished
a ground of responsibility, and inspired a new
hope of life in man who had been made apathetic
by the teachings of fatalism. The subsequent
Oxford movement created simultaneously in
the Anglican Church two counter-currents: one,
reacting from the inconsistent position of semi-
Protestantism, led back to the imperialism of
Rome, — its hierarchical authority, its ecclesiastical system, and its theological dogmatism;
the other, carrying Protestantism forward to its
logical conclusion, led on to the doctrine that
God is a living God, that all men are his chil-

dren, that in every man is a capacity to hear God's voice and to receive his guidance, that the spiritual consciousness may be trusted, and is in the last analysis the seat of authority in religion. And finally, in Puritan England and New England, arose Universalism and Unitarianism, necessary products by reaction against the Puritan theologies: the one affirmed with Calvin that God can make all men righteous, and concluded with inexorable logic that he will, else he would not be a righteous God; the other denied the Augustinian doctrine of native depravity, and declared that man is by creation a Son of God; and from this premise its more advanced section, by a natural though not necessary process of reasoning, passed on to deny altogether any necessity for a redemption divinely revealed, divinely authenticated, and operating with divine efficacy, to bring men into true filial relations with God. These five movements, the Swedenborgian, the Friends, the Methodist, the Broad Church, and the Unitarian and Universalist, all of them drawing more or less from Oriental and Greek sources, have contributed to make that modern revolution in thought which is miscalled the New Theology.

Not less, perhaps more potent than all, has been the influence of modern social and political life. That is characteristically democratic;

not only in government, but in the arts and sciences, in education, and in religion. And an imperial theology cannot permanently remain unmodified in a democratic society.

Nevertheless, this so-called New Theology is neither new nor a theology. It is not absolutely but only relatively new, — new only in contrast with the Puritan theology out of which it has sprung, and from which it is a reaction. It is not truly a theology, since its chief inspiration is a deep desire to get away from the questions of the purely speculative intellect, the answers to which constitute theology, to the practical questions of the Hebrew seers, the answers to which constitute religion. It may be roughly described as largely composed of three elements: a renaissance of Greek thought; a revival of the Hebraic spirit; and a spirit of humanism due to apparently triumphant democracy. Without attempting in this chapter to distinguish the various elements which have contributed to producing it, I endeavor here to give briefly its most characteristic features, describing what it aims to be rather than what it is, that is, describing it as a tendency rather than as a finished product.

The church, then, is coming more and more to conceive of God, not as some one outside of his creation ruling *over* it, but as some one inside

his creation ruling *within* it.   In its material applications this is a familiar truth — God not a
mechanic who has built an engine and stands in
the locomotive and holds the lever, turning off or
on the steam, and regulating the machine as he
will; but God a spirit, and as a spirit indwelling
in all that he has made.   The organist sits at the
instrument and plays upon it.   He is not the
organ.   He ministers it, directs it, controls it.
Presently he stops.   The quartet rise and sing.
They also use organs.   Their own throats are the
organs they use, and they can put into their
music far more of their real spirit, because they
are using themselves, than he can who uses but
the tubes of tin or of wood.   Now, we are coming to think of God as dwelling in nature as
the spirit dwells in the body.   Not that God
and nature are identical; he transcends nature
as I transcend my body, and am more than my
body, and shall live on when my body is dust
and ashes; nevertheless now ruling not over
my body, but in my body.   We are also coming to think of God as ruling, not only in physical nature, but in a somewhat similar manner in human nature.   The king rules *over*
his subjects.   The father rules *in* his children.
The Czar of the Russias does not know those
that are subject to his authority.   He issues
his laws.   They are sent out every whither by

messengers, and executed by subordinates. He
does not and cannot put himself into the Rus-
sians. All he can do is to tell them what they
must do. He cannot transform them into a likeness of himself. But the father, just in the
measure that he is a father, can do this. He
uses authority only as a means to this end. He
does not say to his child, Thou shalt and Thou
shalt not, any further than the infirmity of his
nature compels him to do it. He puts his
own nature into his children. They do not say,
My father has made this law, I must obey it
or suffer; but they come to think as he thinks,
feel as he feels, love what he loves, have the
ambition that he possesses, the purity that he
possesses, the hopes and purposes that he possesses; they become, as we say, "chips of the
old block." Thus the new doctrine of divine
sovereignty transcends the older doctrine. The
conception of God that is *in* man surpasses the
conception of God *over* man. The doctrine of
evolution is not atheistic. The conception of
God in nature and in humanity does not remove
God from humanity. In olden times the Jews
once a year went up to the great Temple to see
their King; subsequently once a week to the synagogue to see their King. But the child of God
lives not under a king whom he can go to see
only once a year or once a week; he lives with

his Father; the child's life is the Father's life, and the child's will is naught save as he brings it into subjection, in every thought, every desire, every aspiration, to the Father's will. What does the bride mean when she promises to *obey* her husband? That the wife is to be the serf and the husband is to rule *over* her? No! But that in the royal realm of love the wife will merge her will with her husband's will, so that, as life flows on, these two wills will become one will in the loyalty of love. The church is not the servant, it is the bride of God.

This new conception of God, as immanent in nature, is necessarily accompanied by a new conception of law and miracles. Rather, we are going back to the New Testament conception and definition of miracles. They are no longer regarded as violations of natural law, or even as suspensions of natural law. Indeed, in strictness of speech, in the view of this philosophy, there are no natural laws to be violated or suspended. There is only one Force, that is God; law is but the habit of God's action; miracles are but the manifestation of his power and presence in unexpected actions, demonstrating the existence of an intelligent Will and Power superior to that of man. I say that this is a recurrence to the New Testament conception and definition of miracles, for the writers of the New

Testament knew nothing about nature and the supernatural, nothing about natural causes and the violation or suspension of natural laws. The words they used to characterize what we call miracles indicate their apprehension of these events. Four words were used by them: "wonders," "powers," "works," and "signs" or "miracles." [1] Any event attracting attention and compelling *wonder*, exhibiting unusual or more than human *power*, accomplishing a real *work*, usually beneficent, and serving as the *sign* of a special messenger and an authentication of his message, is in the conception of the writers of the New Testament a miracle. As the New Theology believes that "all power belongs to God," that God is immanent in the universe, that there is no real distinction between the natural and the supernatural, that the only dualism is the material or physical and the immaterial or spiritual, it has no difficulty in believing that the control of the physical by the spiritual, and therefore of the universe by its God, is sometimes manifested by unexpected or unusual acts of power and wisdom for spiritual ends. These are miracles. Whether any particular event reported as such a witness of divine

[1] The latter word is of course merely the transliteration of the Latin word *miraculum*, the Latin equivalent of *seemeion*, "sign."

power actually took place is purely and simply a question of evidence. The New Theology has no hesitation, therefore, in accepting some miracles and rejecting others: in accepting, for example, the resurrection of Jesus Christ as a fact sufficiently authenticated; doubting the resurrection of the saints at the death of Christ, recorded only by Matthew, as insufficiently authenticated; and disbelieving the historical character of the Jonah legend of the great fish, as not authenticated at all.

As we are coming to think of God *in* men, not *over* men, so we are coming to think of the laws which God issues as in himself and in man, not apart from himself and over man: not less inviolable, but more inviolable; not less certain, but more certain; not as laws apart from man to which he must subject himself, but laws wrought into his nature and the very constitution of his being. We speak of laws of the State. They have been enacted by our legislators, some good, some bad, some indifferent. We speak of the laws of art, the laws of music, the laws of political economy, the laws of history. They have not been enacted by a legislative body. They are not statutes that have been enacted over art, over music, over industry; they are inherent in the very nature of art, of music, of literature, of industry, of politics. Whether God wrote the

Ten Commandments with his finger in the stone or not, and whatever that strange enigmatical declaration means, he wrote them in the very nature of man when he made man. They are not something God has issued, saying, You must obey this: they are something God has wrought into the very fibre and structure of man's being. These laws are laws of man because they are the laws of God, and laws of God because they are laws of man, and because man and God are in very essence one. The laws of the sunbeam are the laws of the sun, because the sunbeam comes from the sun, bringing the laws of the sun and the nature of the sun, that it may warm and vivify the earth. And the laws of my nature are the laws of God's own nature because I come from God, have God's nature written in my members, and am a child of God, possessing my Father's nature. They are wrought into the very fibre and structure of the human soul; inviolable, not because a divine imperial authority, sitting above, looks out on all the earth, and sees every violation and follows it with arrest and punishment, — inviolable, because they are inherent in the nature of man and inherent in the nature of God; so absolute and so inviolable, that if we could conceive that God himself were dethroned and ceased to exist, law would still go on throughout eternity, unless nature itself were dissolved into anarchy.

Hence, revelation is not a book external to men, giving laws which are external to men, by a God who is external to men. Revelation is the unveiling in human consciousness of that which God wrote in the human soul when he made it. In the spring I go to my garden bed, and write in the soil with my finger certain letters, and sow the proper seeds and cover them over, and there is nothing but a bed of mould. In June, from these seeds flowers will have sprung up, and they will have spelled out a name. The sun has revealed them. They were there, but the sun has made that to appear which but for the shining of the sun would not have appeared. So, in the heart of man God has written his message, his inviolable law and his merciful redemption, because he has made the heart of man akin to the heart of God. Revelation is the upspringing of this life of law and love, of righteousness and mercy, under the influence of God's own personal presence and power. The question between the two schools of theology concerning the Bible is thus important and even fundamental. It is not whether there are some specks of sandstone in the marble. To the Old Theology, God, as a great infinite Cæsar ruling the world, has framed certain statutes and given them to us, and we must obey them, or come into collision with him and suffer the threatened penalties. To the New Theology, he has made man after his own image and written his own nature in the human conscience and in human love, and then has interpreted by the mouth of his prophets what he has written in the hearts of his children.

Such a revelation is not infallible; but it is for that very reason the more perfect revelation. It is said, If you think that the gold and the earth are mixed together in the Bible, how will you discriminate, how will you tell what is gold and what is earth? We do not wish to discriminate; we do not wish to separate. It is not gold with dross; it is oxygen with nitrogen. The oxygen is mixed with the nitrogen in order that it may the better be breathed, and the better minister to human life. In the Bible the divine is mingled — inextricably and indivisibly mingled — with the human, that humanity may receive it and be ministered to by it. We cannot take the great truths of God and his government and his love into our own experiences except as they are woven into the experience of men of like passions and infirmities and imperfections as ourselves. The Bible is a more sacred book because it is a human book. It is a diviner book, not merely because it shows us the law of God and the nature of God, but because it shows us God and man inextricably woven together so that they cannot be separated. It is impossible to run a knife of cleavage through the character of Jesus Christ, and say, "This was God, and this man." The glory of Christ's revelation of God to men is that he shows that God and man are so interwoven that separation is impossible. That which is true of incarnation is true of revelation; the divine glory of the Bible is that the truth and love and life and glory of God show themselves in human experience. Thus the Bible becomes not an end, but a means to an end. It is the glass in and through which we see God darkly. And all the better because darkly. If the glass were not smoked, we could not see the sun at all. Our faith is not in the book, but in the God to whom they bear witness whose lives and teachings are revealed in the book. We first hear the echo in prophet and epistle; then we listen for the Voice itself. Thus we follow our fathers, but it is that we may come to the Presence to which they came. The wings of God's own angels are over us, and the very presence of God himself is in our heart, and his eyes look love into our eyes, and his life is filling our life, and we will not go back to the portico of the Temple and the echo of the Voice.

Faith in God has gradually brought with it faith in man as the son of God; and faith in the

power of man, — not of a few mystics, or especially elected saints, or divinely appointed priests
and prophets, — but faith in the power of man,
and of every man, as a son of God, to know
God directly and immediately. Imperialism in
theology necessarily carried with it rationalism.
Immanence in theology necessarily carries with
it intuitionalism. In the United States, in the
death of Dr. Emmons, in 1840, there died the
last representative of the old school of New
England preachers, the purely logical. A new
school is taking its place, the intuitional. That
man is a reasonable creature; that the reason is
the supreme and divine faculty; that his reason
is to be convinced by the truth; that when his
reason is convinced his will must obey; that
when this result is reached he is a converted being — this was the philosophy which, sometimes
avowed, sometimes unrecognized, underlay the
preaching of the old school. The whole fabric
of the religious life was built by logical processes, by means of doctrine, on the human reason. But all men are not logical; and all men
do not obey the truth, even when it is made
clear to their logical understanding. The office
of logic is to criticise rather than to enforce, and
to enforce rather than to reveal. Spiritual truth
is not mined by picks and beaten out by ham-
mers. It is in the heavens, not buried in the

earth; to be seen, not mined.   It is within, not
without; not to be arrived at by slow processes
of deduction, but to be apprehended and appre-
ciated upon a mere presentation of it.   This far-
reaching truth was spoken outside the church,
in England by a Carlyle, and in America by an
Emerson; its spiritual prophet in the Puritan
churches of New England was Horace Bushnell.
That truth is immediately and directly seen by
the soul; that God is no best hypothesis to account for the phenomena of creation, but the
soul's best friend, its Father, its intimate personal
companion; that inspiration is no remote phe-
nomenon, once attested by miracles, now forever
silenced in the grave of a dead God, but a universal and eternal communion between a living
God and living souls; that the forgiveness of sins
is infinitely more than any theory of atonement,
and that no theory of atonement can comprehend
the full meaning of forgiveness of sins — these
were not the theories of a philosopher; they were
the realities, the vital convictions, the personal
experiences of the saint, whose sainthood must be
in the heart of the critic before he can criticise
and in the heart of the disciple before he can
comprehend.

Thus the New Theology, breaking away from
the external and governmental conceptions of
Romanism, and through a revival of Orientalism

getting a more spiritual conception of the teaching of the New Testament, uses both the church and the Bible as instruments for creating in the heart of men in the nineteenth century the same spiritual life which the Bible portrays in the hearts of the patriarchs and the prophets of olden time, and develops a style of preaching which appeals directly and immediately to the divine in humanity, and speaks with authority, because it evokes the authority of the divinity which is in every man.

As the Latin or Puritan system of theology gave a conception of God, of law, and of revelation as external, so it represented sin, though less consistently, as external. For its conception of sin was, substantially, that there is a great King who is absolutely righteous, and who has issued certain laws which ought to be obeyed, and that men have set their will against the will of this great King, and have deliberately determined that they will not do what he commands them to do. But, inasmuch as a great number, if not the great majority, of men are utterly unconscious of having set their will deliberately against the will of God, or of being in any wise in rebellion against him, this theology ran back the history of sin to a supposed origin in a remote past; it said there was a progenitor of this whole human race to whom this edict was given, who disobeyed it, and that in his sin we all sinned, and in his fall we all fell. By that one act the whole human race was brought into rebellion against God. We have accordingly, it was said, a state of society resembling that which existed in our Southern States twenty-five or more years ago. The world is in rebellion against God, and, although individuals may not have directly enlisted against the Almighty, they have been swept along by the current into this rebellion, and are really, even if unconsciously, rebels against him and his government and laws.

Three different causes are at work undermining this theological system which makes sin for the race rest fundamentally upon one act of apostasy by a progenitor in some remote past. Evolution declares that the human race has not fallen from a higher estate to a lower, but is climbing from a lower estate to a higher. Modern Biblical critics maintain that the story of the Fall is not and does not claim to be a revelation, but is a spiritualized account of an ancient legend or myth, to be found in other literature at least as ancient as the most ancient date attributed by any scholar to the author of Genesis. And students in sociology have discovered that the cause of crime is not a strong and rebellious will, but a weak and irresolute one. It does not follow that modern thought is coming to the conclusion that there is no real sin in the human race, no penalty following sin, and no need of forgiveness and redemption to deliver from both sin and penalty. On the contrary, I think we are coming to have a deeper and a diviner sense of sin; a truer and a more practical conception of what sin is, and in what it does really consist. The laws of God are laws written in the human soul, and the sin of man is a sin against the law of his own nature. Sin is not man setting himself against a law external to himself. Every man is two men; every man is a battle-ground in which the higher and the lower man are contending one against the other. Man has come up out of the lower condition, and in every new stage of his life he comes under a new and a diviner law, the law of a new and a diviner nature. He is no longer under the laws of his old being. The very standards of truth and righteousness change. In every new stage of evolution he comes under a new law of righteousness. Men are coming step by step into a higher and spiritual realm, and under the authority of a higher and spiritual law. Sin is a relapse. Depravity lies in those elements of the old nature which makes such a relapse always a possible and real danger. "If ye were blind," says Christ, "ye should

have no sin : but now ye say, We see; therefore
your sin remaineth." It is as we come up into
the light that sin becomes possible. If there
were no redemption, there would be no sin.

I can remember, when a boy, how the minister
used to exhort me to lay down the weapons of
my rebellion. I did not know what he meant.
I had no weapons of rebellion. I thought I was
doubly wicked because I did not see that I was
a rebel, though in very truth I cannot, looking
back along my life, remember the time when I
did not sincerely, in my deepest heart of hearts,
desire to know the will of God and do the will
of God. No! I am not a rebel, and never have
been. I repeat the language of the Episcopa-
lian Confession: "I have done the things which
I ought not to have done, and I have left undone the things which I ought to have done."
True! and yet, after all, if my Father were to
stop me, and say, "Make your inventory; tell
me what things you did yesterday that you ought
not to have done," I should often find it difficult to put my finger on one of them; "Tell
me what things you left undone yesterday that
you ought to have done," I might not easily put
my finger even on one of those. But when I
come to the closing sentence of that triple declaration, "There is no health in me," it is in no
figurative sense that I feel like putting my hand

on my mouth and my mouth in the dust, and crying out, "Woe unto me, for I am unclean." It is not the things which I have done, it is not the things which I have left undone, that call me to repentance. It is the kind of being I am. I have not stained my hand with the blood of my neighbor. I have not put my hand into his pocket and filched his earnings. But, when I look into my heart, and see what there is of ambition and pride and selfishness and greed still hiding there, I do not know but that, if I had lived where my brother lives, my hand would be red as his is, my hand would be smirched with greed as his has been. I am haunted by another self. I hate no man except myself. And when this shadowy monster walks by my side and whispers the evil suggestion into my ear, I long to get my hand upon his throat and my feet upon his prostrate person! It is not what I have done; it is not what I have left undone: it is what there is left in me, that came I know not whence, that is here I know not why, and that somehow must be cleansed away before I am the man, God helping me, I mean to be.[1]

As we are coming, then, to think of sin not as successive acts of the will performed, and cer-

[1] This subject is more fully treated in a subsequent chapter on "The Evolution of the Individual Soul."

tainly not as some great apostasy in the past in which we had no share, but as in elements of our being which are unworthy of those that are called the children of God, so we are coming to see that penalty is not external penalty inflicted by a governor for crime perpetrated. The law is in ourselves; the disease and the disorder are in ourselves; and the penalty is in ourselves. Every sin comes back to plague the sinner. There is no need of any flagellations; every man flagellates himself. No God in heaven or devil in hell is needed to kindle the fire that is not quenched, or to breed the worm that dieth not. Every man kindles the fire and breeds the worm in his own soul. This is not new. The old Greek tragedians saw it, and wrought it into their tragedies. Dante saw it, and repeated it in the story of the Inferno. Shakespeare saw it, and revealed it in Macbeth and in Othello. Browning and Tennyson have seen and interpreted it. That penalty and sin are both within the man; that we never enter into heaven, but heaven into us; that we never enter into hell, but hell into us — this, the vision of the poets, pagan and Christian, the church is beginning slowly and after long years of miseducation to appropriate and make its own. How this self-indulgent appetite vitiates and destroys the very tissues of the body and makes impossible the simple, natural, healthful pleasures of the physical organization! How this grasping, greedy, covetous appetite grows by what it feeds on, until the man is consumed by the fire of his own insatiable lust for wealth! How this pride walls the man in, and isolates him, and separates him from his fellows; how it incrusts him, and turns him from a living man into stone! And this vanity that makes us desire the applause of our fellow-men, and puffs us up with conceit, how it deprives us of the pleasure we seek in the very process of our striving for their applause, and brings us into contempt in the very act by which we strive to gratify our vanity! Nay, how all these sins isolate us from one another, and isolate us from God! Men build themselves into narrow cells, inflict upon themselves the penalty of a perpetual solitary confinement, go out of the brotherhood, and estrange themselves from their heavenly Father. No Peter stands at the heavenly gate to say who may come in and who may not. The gates of the Heavenly City are flung wide open day and night, and when men die they may go straight up to that gate and walk in — if they wish. But as men that dive to the bottom of the sea incase themselves in armor, and then going down are untouched by the sea, we, by our pride, our selfishness, **our vanity**, our self-conceit, our appetites, so incase ourselves that, standing in the midst of purity and light and life, we are untouched by it, solitary in the kingdom of God on earth, solitary in the kingdom of God in heaven.

If forgiveness of sin were taking away an external penalty threatened by an imperial God upon men for violation of an external law, then it could be taken away externally. But if penalty is sin and sin is penalty, if these are only two aspects of the same thing, different ways of spelling, as it were, the same word, then redemption must be within, as the penalty is within and as the lawlessness is within. The man who is a battle-ground between the animal and the spiritual can find peace only in one of two ways: either he must go back to the animal or he must go up to the heavenly. The man in whose nature appetite is struggling with self-respect and conscience must go back to the abyss or up to the Son of God, or remain torn in sunder eternally by these two conflicting motives that are within his soul. God himself cannot take the penalty out of a life and leave the sin in, unless he were to revolutionize the nature of man and his own nature. What God is doing in the world is not lifting off the threatened penalty from men that have done something wrong, but putting life into men who are as yet only half

living, and taking the death out of men that are
still half dead. There is not one single passage
in the New Testament that in explicit terms
promises remission of penalty; but the Bible
is written all over its pages with the radiant
promise of the remission of sins. The function
and aim of the gospel is to take the pride, the
passion, the selfishness, the vanity, the vice, the
sensuality, and whatever other evil thing there
may be, out of the heart and out of the life.
Redemption is within, not without. It is healing. Not uncommon in forensic theology is the
figure of the sinner shut up in his prison-house,
and the messenger coming with the word of pardon signed and sealed in the blood of Christ,
and the promise, If the prisoner will accept this
pardon in faith and repentance, he may go free.
But no such figure is found in the Bible. What
are the figures there? They are such as these:
Your sins are a cloud in the heavens; like the
shining of the sun on the cloud is the shining of
the life of God on the heart, and he will shine
on, until he has blotted out every sin. Sin is
like a record in a book; he will with chemicals
erase the record and make the page white and
ready for a new writing. The life is like that
lived in some preëxisting state; the man may
be born again. Man is a slave to sin; God
will set him free. Man is in his grave, and

such corruption has taken hold of him that other men say, "Do not go near him, he is so corrupt; leave him to himself;" but Christ comes and stands at the grave and says: "Lazarus, come forth." To be redeemed is to come forth, now, out of that corruption, out of that darkness, into the bright shining of the sun, into the singing of the birds, into the immortal life that is here and now, the life with God and in God. The New Theology is not the doctrine that men need no forgiveness and no God to forgive them. It is profoundly the reverse; it is the doctrine that sin is wrought into the very fibre and structure of man, that penalty is a part of the sin and must exist so long as sin is there, and that forgiveness is casting the sin out and putting new life in.

And so incarnation is not merely a coming of God to man, it is a dwelling of God in man. Universalism and Unitarianism were the natural, if not the logical and necessary, conclusions of Calvinism. They were bred in the Puritan atmosphere. They grew in the Puritan community. They were Presbyterian in Old England and Congregational in New England. They have never grown out of Methodism. Let the world believe that God is sovereign in any such sense as that man has no sovereignty left, and that whether he shall remain in sin and misery throughout eternity depends wholly upon God, and in no wise upon the individual man, — then whenever the world comes also to believe that God is love, it will inevitably believe also in a universal salvation. Let the world think that God is on his throne apart from man, that what he is doing for men he is doing externally for them, that a great gulf exists between God and man, that they are not of kin, that man's nature is not divine, is indeed undivine, and it will inevitably come to think of the Christ coming to earth as a messenger with an embassage from the sovereign to the rebels, telling them the terms on which humanity may be pardoned. But, on the other hand, let the world and the church come to believe that law and revelation and sin and redemption are all written in man, and it will come to write another word in man, and that word Incarnation, — God coming into one life in order that he may come into all lives; into one human experience, in order that he may enter into all human experiences; Christ the door through which and by which man enters into God and God enters into man. As in the spring the first lily of the season puts its white head above the ground, then drops its head that it may whisper to its seed sisters, saying to them, "Come, come! this is what you are meant to be," so into the darkness of a pagan night, and into the vileness of a wholly earthly history, came the one transcendent, pure, divine figure, standing for those few short years upon the earth, showing what is truly God by showing what is truly man when God is in him, and calling out to us, still in the earthiness, still in the darkness, and saying to us, "Come! this is what you were meant to be, this is what God is trying to make you, this is what your aspirations mean. You are sons of God; the law of his nature is the law of your nature; and, working with him and letting him work in you, you shall come out into the sunlight of God's own love and become the sharer of his own life."

If we cannot state philosophically, and cannot even see quite clearly, how it is that the sacrifice of Christ works out this divine redemption in the human soul, at least we can see that there is no such Christian redemption except through the ministry of suffering. It is not that man is sacrificed to appease God — it is God who is sacrificed to redeem man. Christ could not have revealed a God of truth and not have been a teaching Christ; nor revealed a God of life and not have been a living Christ, carrying out in life the principles he inculcated; nor revealed a God of love and not have been a suffering Christ, for love must suffer so long as the loved one sins. Christ — who came that he might reveal the nature and heart of God, who came that he might show us God in man, helping man toward God — came to mingle his tears with our tears, and, sinless though he was, his vicarious repentance and his death *to* sin with our death *in* sin, in order that he might make it clear to us that God is always suffering and struggling and laboring with us. In the wonderful statue of the Laocoön, — the father and the two children, one on either side, and the serpents who have come up out of the sea to destroy them, — the father is fighting the serpents, not for his own life, but for his sons' lives. But the struggle and the anguish in their faces are less than in his, for love's battle is hotter and love's suffering greater than the battle and the suffering of self. So out of that dark past, out of that animal nature, out of that strange mystery from which we were called by the creative word of God, who makes us of clay, yet breathes the breath of his own life into us, come the serpentine elements that are in our own complex nature, as if to strangle all that is divine and truly manly in us; and it is our Father who is with us, and whose reflected image we see in the cross. The agony in the soul of the Christ is but the reflection of the sorrow that is in the Father's soul. Every

burden of our life is in his life, and he wrestles
for us and will conquer for us. It is not the
omniscience nor the omnipotence of God that is
most unfathomable, but his mercy, his sympathy, his love; the sympathy of a God who is in
such touch with humanity that we never commit a sin that he does not feel the shame of it,
and we never feel a remorse that the bitterness
of it does not enter into him, and we never
know a sorrow that he does not sit down with
us in our grief, and we are never lifted up with
a great joy that he is not joyful also. For not
by the suffering only, but by the joy also; not
by the struggle only, but by the peace also; by
the whole entering of God into human life, his
life becomes our life, and we are made partakers of his nature, because he comes down and
makes himself partaker with us in our lives.

Thus the New Theology is evolved out of the
Old Theology, and the same spiritual faith is in
them both. We believe that God is an absolute, supreme King; but we know this King to
be our Father, in personal relations with each
one of us. We believe his laws are absolute,
and not to be broken; but they are his laws because they are the laws of his own nature, and
our laws because they are the laws of our nature,
for we are the children of God and have come
from him. We believe in a revelation that is

written in a unique book, with a unique character
and a unique history; but we believe that the
writings in this book are but the reflection of
that which was written by God in the inmost
being of the prophets, and we see the vision better because we see it reflected from a mirror and
in enigma. We believe in the awfulness of sin;
not chiefly in the things which we have done, not
chiefly in the things which we have left undone,
but in the weakness, the infirmity, the animal-
ism, the unworthiness that is in us, and that
might sweep us out any moment into the abyss
from which the hand of Providence has thus far
guarded us. We believe in the certainty of
punishment, not because by and by we shall be
heard before an omniscient Judge; but because
in man's own conscience is erected a judgment
seat from which he never can escape unless he
flies from his own nature. We believe in a
great redemption; not one that opens the door
of a prison and lets us out, but one that opens
the door of our own self-erected prison and lets
Christ in, and so fulfils in us the prayer of Tennyson,

> "Oh, for a man to arise in me,
> That the man that I am may cease to be!"

We believe in a sacrifice, not of a mediator to
appease the wrath of God, but of God manifest
in the flesh, sacrificing himself to purify and
perfect the children of men.

CHAPTER V.

THE EVOLUTION OF THE CHURCH.

JESUS CHRIST was the founder neither of religion nor of *a* religion. If religion be the life of God in the soul of man, that existed long before Jesus Christ came into the world. Not to go outside of Judaism, it was seen in Abraham, Moses, David, Isaiah, and the long line of patriarchs and prophets of Jewish history. If religion be such a manifestation of God as produces a moral influence on the life and character of man, that also had existed, both within and without Judaism, long prior to the time of Christ. Jesus Christ was not, therefore, the founder of religion. It was founded in the beginning, when God created man in his own image and breathed into him the breath of a spiritual life. Nor was he the founder of *a* religion. A religion, as distinguished from religion, is a particular and organized type of the life of God in the soul of man. It is a particular form of moral and spiritual organization, resulting from some specialized perception of that manifestation of God to man which is as universal as the race. Each religion has therefore its own specific expression or embodiment: an intellectual expression in a creed or theological system; an emotional expression in a ritual or liturgy; and an organic expression in an institution or institutions. Christ gave to his disciples neither a creed, a liturgy, nor rules for the construction of an ecclesiastical organization. He has told us very distinctly for what he came into the world. "I have come," he said, "that they might have life, and that they might have it more abundantly." "I give unto them eternal life." "Father, thou hast given thy Son power over all flesh, that he should give eternal life to as many as thou hast given him." He came that he might give life, and this life has expressed itself in intellectual forms, that is in creeds; in emotional forms, that is in liturgies; in institutional forms, that is in churches. But he gave neither a creed, a liturgy, nor a church to the world.

He assumed certain truths and gave expression to them as truths of vital experience, but he never crystallized them into a creed. Thus he was accustomed to address God as his Father, and he told his disciples to do the same. He illustrated the relationship between God and man by that between a benignant father and an erring child. He said that God was more ready to impart his holy influence to those that desired

it than an earthly father to give good gifts to his
children.   But he never described the attributes
of God, nor afforded any theological definition of
God, nor discussed philosophically the character
of the Infinite One, or his relations to the finite
creation.   He assumed that men were bound
together by a deeper relationship than that which
finds expression in church, state, or even race.
He passed beyond all these boundaries within
which we still, for the most part, confine our
sympathies.   He skillfully awakened human regard, even in the breast of a narrow-minded Jew,
for the renegade, apostate, and heretical Samaritan, by picturing such an one with a compas-
sionate and tender heart.   But one looks in vain
in his sayings for a definition of human brotherhood or a systematic philosophy of society.   He
treated men habitually as possessing immortal
natures, — treated life here as a fragment whose
consequences are projected into the hereafter;
but he never discussed the doctrine of immortality, much less the specific conditions of the
future state.   One may, perhaps, out of his sayings construct a Christian doctrine of Last
Things, but he will have to construct it himself;
he will not find it in the Gospels made ready to
his hand.   Jesus Christ lived at a time and in
a country when sacrifices were the universal
expression of worship, and access to God and

relief from the burden and remorse of sin were supposed possible only through the shedding of blood. He said nothing against this sacrificial system, but when he saw in men the signs of a genuine repentance, he simply bade them go in peace and sin no more. He assumed that there was a provision by which the burdened soul might find peace, and that all that was necessary for that purpose was to abandon the sin and enter upon a new life. A doctrine of atonement may be deduced from his teaching, — has been deduced from his teaching, — but the doctrine of the atonement is a deduction. Christ nowhere gives expression to it in a philosophical or doctrinal form. He assumed a position toward mankind of calm superiority. He never classed himself with men. He never expressed repentance for sin, or aspiration for a purer life. He acted as one who had come out of a great fullness to impart to humanity in its great poverty. And yet the doctrine of the Person of Christ, though not stated in the teachings of Christ, may be deduced from them. That he left his claim to divinity unformulated, to be made for him by his followers, rather than by him for himself, is evident from a single significant circumstance. When he was put on trial for his life, it was impossible to find two witnesses who could agree together concerning any utterance

of Jesus Christ which even a partial and preju-
diced court could construe into an explicit claim
of divinity; humanly speaking, it may safely
be said that Christ could not have been condemned for blasphemy, even by the corrupt
court of Caiaphas, had he not consented to be
put upon the stand himself and to have the oath
administered to him, and then and there, under the solemn sanction of that oath, and with
the death penalty hanging over him as the result, declared that he was the Son of God, and
would come in the clouds of glory to judge the
world.

As Jesus Christ formulated no creed, that is,
no intellectual expression of the religious life,
so he formulated no liturgy, that is, no emotional expression of the religious life.   He was
accustomed to pray, though generally in private.
On at least one occasion, however, he met with
his disciples and united with them in a simple
service of prayer and praise about the Passover
table.   Once they asked him to give them a
liturgy.   He answered in an incomparable form
of prayer which includes the common wants of
humanity, its need of food, of forgiveness, and
of guidance, expressed in three very simple petitions; but that neither he nor his disciples
laid stress upon the form of words is evident
from the fact that the form differs in the two

reports which have been preserved for us, while the indications are that the prayer itself was in part, at least, composed of petitions which were before current in Jewish worship. The Jews were accustomed to baptize proselytes from heathen communities, as a token that the baptized washed away their old superstitions and entered a new life; John the Baptist, seizing on this familiar rite, declared that the Jews as well as pagans needed purification, and he used baptism to enforce this teaching. Some of Christ's disciples followed John's example, and Christ, after his resurrection, bade them use this symbol among all people, regardless of race, and as a form of initiation, not into Judaism, nor into a sect of reformed Jews, but into a universal and divine fellowship. The birthday of the Jewish nation was celebrated by a great festival, one feature of it being a supper. Jesus Christ bade his followers in the future remember him whenever they thus celebrated their nation's birthday. In neither case did he create or institute a ceremonial; he simply gave a new and deeper significance and direction to one already familiar. In brief, Jesus Christ inspired his disciples with reverence, with aspiration, with thanksgiving, with love; but he left them to express that spiritual life which he had imparted to them in language of their own.

In a similar manner he organized no institutions of religion. Early in his ministry, he called about him from his followers twelve to be his more immediate companions. A little later he sent them out two by two, to tell the people in the villages and rural districts that the Kingdom of God was at hand, while he carried the same message to the towns and cities. Subsequently he retreated from the crowd which thronged about him in Galilee, and seeking retirement with these twelve, devoted several weeks to giving them instruction concerning the spirit which should actuate them and the principles which should guide them, in carrying on his work after he was gone. Still later, in a wider district, with a more scattered population, he sent out seventy itinerant prophets on an evangelistic mission. After his death and resurrection, he met those who had remained loyal to him, and told them to continue their ministry, and to carry unto others the new life which they had received from him. But he organized no society, formulated no constitution, appointed no officers, prescribed no rules. He left the life to create its own ecclesiastical organization, as he left it to find its own intellectual and emotional expression.

The reason for this is not far to seek. Paul has explicitly stated it. Prophecies, he says, shall fail, tongues shall cease, knowledge shall vanish away, but faith, hope, love, abide forever. Even inspired teaching, and all the forms in which it may utter itself, and all the articulated knowledge of which it is the expression, are evanescent. These are phenomena, and phenomena always are and always must be transitory. What abides, — what only can abide, — is life. It was this life which Jesus Christ came to impart, the life of faith, looking through visible things as through a veil, to the invisible glory which the visible at once conceals and discloses; the life of hope looking forward and upward in the expectation of a to-morrow that shall be better than to-day; the life of love seeking not its own welfare, but the welfare of others. This threefold spirit is eternal and constant, while all expressions of this threefold spirit are transitory and changeful. Christ instituted no ecclesiastical organism, framed no constitution, prescribed no rules, appointed no officers; but he gave in various ways expression to this spirit of faith, and hope, and love, as a spirit that must embody itself in a church which after his death should carry on his work.

But he did more than this.

The Jews in the Wilderness had instituted a Great Congregation which assembled on certain occasions for the determination of great national questions. Whether the Jewish commonwealth was a free democracy and all the people assembled for the purpose of mutual conference and public decision, or whether it was a republic and this Great Congregation was a representative body is not altogether certain. Probably in the earlier history it was a popular assembly, in the later history a representative assembly. It was, at all events, the representative of the nation, and its action reflected the national will. In the Greek version of the Scriptures the name Ecclesia, meaning the Called Forth, was given to this assembly. The same name was given in Greece to an analogous assembly of the people for national consultation and common action. Christ implied that his followers were to constitute themselves into such an Ecclesia or assembly. The principles which he indicated as essential to its existence and efficiency are these: —

1. There was to be a church, that is, a gathering together, of all loyal followers of the Master. The bond which was to unite this assembly in one great brotherhood was to be loyalty, — not to a creed, not to an order or an organization, but to a Person, and that Person himself.

The sole condition of admission to this brotherhood while Christ lived was personal loyalty to him. In no solitary instance did he ask any would-be disciple what he believed, or where or how he worshiped, or to what nation or religion he belonged.[1] He simply asked, Are you willing to enter my school and learn of me; enter my kingdom and obey my directions? He was equally willing to welcome to his organization the devout John, the rough, sailor-like, profane Peter, the publican Matthew, the pagan centurion. On the other hand, the scribe who would follow him provided he might first go back to his home to bury his father, or bid his kinsfolk good-by; the ruler of the synagogue who would join him, provided he might still keep the control and administration of his own wealth; the Nicodemus, master in Israel, who was interested in his teaching but thought himself in no need of a new life, were rejected. And when crowds thronged about him with a great enthusiasm, he turned to them and declared that unless they loved him more than father or mother or life itself, they were not worthy of him. If they would be his followers, they must take up the cross daily and follow him. He required of those within the church the same spirit of absolute and unquestioning loyalty. When one of

[1] The case of the Syro-Phœnician woman (Mark vii. 24–30) may be thought to be an exception; but she was not seeking to enter Christ's body of followers as herself a follower, and it is clear from the context that Christ's first refusal to cure her daughter was because granting the cure sought for was sure to destroy that rest and privacy which he was seeking.

his best friends rebuked him for foretelling his own crucifixion, he vouchsafed no explanation, but turned upon the recalcitrant disciple with a sharp rebuke. "Get thee behind me, Satan," he said. When two other friends came to ask for honorable position in the coming kingdom, he answered with a test of their loyalty, "Are ye able to drink of the cup that I shall drink of, and to be baptized with the baptism that I am baptized with?" He sat down at the table with his disciples, no one of whom had thought to offer his services in washing the soiled feet of the others, or even of the Master himself, When he rose, girded himself as a slave, and proceeded with basin and towel to wash and wipe the feet of the disciples, and one protested, he answered simply, I will give you no explanation; you must submit or leave the discipleship. When, after his resurrection, he foretold the martyrdom of Peter, and Peter asked, What shall befall John? the only reply was, "What is that to thee? Follow thou me." Nor was this loyalty to him a temporary condition of the little band, continuing only while the Master was living. On the contrary, he declared explicitly before his death that he would continue to be with his disciples; that he and his Father would come and dwell with them; that the spirit that abode in him should abide with them also;

that it should interpret to them the meaning of his teaching, and open to them new truths which they had not yet been able to receive; that it should impart to them power; and that under this impartation they should do greater works even than those which he had done. Near the close of his life he gave in a beautiful parable an illustration of this principle of spiritual unity in personal loyalty to him as a living Lord and Master. He was just about going out with his friends to a vineyard outside the city walls, or perhaps had already reached this coveted retirement. A vine was growing against the wall; the pruning knife had been at work and some dead branches lay upon the ground. Behold, he said, the symbol of your future life. I am the vine, and shall always be with you. Loyalty to me, fellowship with me, unity with me, is the one condition of our order and our organization. So long as this loyalty is maintained, you will bear fruit; whenever this loyalty is lost, whenever for my will you substitute your own and for my life your independent and individual life, you will be like these branches, cut off from the vine and thrown upon the ground; there will be no life in you. The first principle of his church, the sole secret of its unity, was to be personal loyalty to himself.

2. The second great principle of his church

was that of equality. This future organization was to be a brotherhood of equals. In it there were to be no ranks and orders for the exercise of authority. In the world without, he said, the great and strong dominate the rest. In your organization it shall not be so. You are to acknowledge no Master except myself; all ye are brethren. Offices there may be, but they shall exist, not for honor and emulation, nor for the exercise of authority, but only for service. "He that is greatest among you shall be your servant." More than once the disciples engaged in hot discussion among themselves as to which should be greatest, and strove for precedence. It was after one of these questions that he administered that stinging rebuke, to which I have just referred, by himself washing the feet of the disciples who had been quarreling upon the question which should have the place of honor at the table. On another similar occasion he asked them what had been the subject of their contention, and getting no answer, took a child, and set him in the midst of them, and said, Except ye be converted and become as a little child, ye shall not enter into the kingdom of heaven. This fundamental principle, that every one in his church is responsible directly to God and under no authority except for purposes of service, he illustrated by a pregnant figure which has been singularly misinterpreted by one section of his church. In the East, a key is not unfrequently given to the steward of an estate as the symbol of his authority, much as a bunch of keys is sometimes given to the housekeeper in England, and by her worn, hanging from the waist. I give unto each one of you, he said, the keys of the kingdom of heaven. You are to have authority over yourselves. Whatsoever you prohibit shall be prohibited for you, and whatsoever you permit shall be permitted for you. For you are called unto liberty and self-control. [1]

3. The third principle of his church was that of liberty. In his kingdom no force should be used. Its only appeal should be to the conscience; its only instrument, truth. In the very beginning of his ministry he was tempted to adopt world methods in order to win power, and he peremptorily refused. Later, the people in their enthusiasm would have crowned him King; he refused the coronation and departed from them. He told his disciples that they were not to resist injustice by force. When he was about to be arrested, and one of the disciples would

---

[1] Observe that in this famous passage Christ does not say *whom*soever, but *what*soever. Observe also that the kingdom of heaven is in the language of Christ a kingdom of God upon the earth.

have resisted, he bade his impetuous friend put up his sword. When he stood before Pilate and was questioned, Art thou a king? he replied, I am, but a king whose only authority is the truth, and whose only followers are those who acknowledge supreme allegiance to the truth. And in telling his disciples how they were to act in the church towards those who refused to acknowledge its decisions, he said, Let such an one "be unto thee as an heathen man and a publican." That is, let him go his way, have nothing more to do with him. They were not to attempt to coerce him. He was to have his liberty; they were to have theirs.

At the death of Jesus Christ, the disciples went forth to carry the new life which they had received from their Master, the life of faith and hope and love, into a world which was sensual, despairing, and cruelly selfish. At first, they made no attempt to form any ecclesiastical organization. They had no conception how long and weary a time must elapse before the kingdom of God would arrive which they believed their Master had come to usher in. They fully expected his return during their lifetime. They conceived no need of any society which should outlast a single generation. The organizations which sprang up out of the apostolic preaching were spontaneous in their origin and different from one another in their form and structure, though at first essentially the same in their spirit. The early disciples had no regular places of worship; they often met in private homes; their societies were in their nature what they were sometimes called, households of faith. Occasionally an entire Jewish synagogue would accept the new faith. Then the organization remained unchanged, while the spirit which animated it was revolutionized. Sometimes the brotherhood was composed chiefly of converted pagans; then the organization naturally fell into the forms and methods with which the pagans were familiar. These households of faith, whether Jewish or pagan in their social origin, had no creed, no organized system of theology, no established liturgy. But they believed in a Messiah to whose second coming in their own generation they all joyfully looked forward; they used the Hebrew psalmody both for praise and for their responsive readings, as in the Jewish liturgies; they employed the Lord's Prayer, though in connection with extemporaneous prayer; they made the worship subordinate to instruction; they gathered frequently, if not every week, about a supper-table, in commemoration of their Lord's death and in joyful anticipation of his return; this they followed sometimes with a church supper, partly as an occasion of social fellowship, partly as a means for providing the poor with food out of the resources of the more wealthy; and they used baptism, generally, if not always, by immersion, as a rite of initiation into the new brotherhood, at first with the simple formula "In the name of the Lord Jesus Christ," — subsequently with the formula now generally in use, "In the name of the Father, the Son, and the Holy Spirit." But the principles of which I have spoken were characteristic of all these primitive households. That is, the one condition of their unity was loyalty to the Master; and this loyalty to one Master carried with it the liberty of an absolute and an equal brotherhood.

The Roman empire was founded on principles directly antagonistic to those propounded by Jesus Christ. That empire was organized upon the principle of absolute subservient obedience to the emperor: his will was the source of all law; belief in him was the Roman's sole creed; reverence for him was the Roman's sole religion. To him altars were raised in every household; from him was derived the only authority which the Roman recognized. And this authority was exhibited and exercised through an elaborate bureaucracy. There was no brotherhood, and no semblance of brotherhood. Absolutism was filtered down through successive subalterns to the remotest province and to the minutest affairs of the great empire. And this authority, centring in the emperor and expressed and exercised through ranks and orders of subordinates, was enforced by physical penalties. The ground of this authority was not in conscience, but in fear. Rome was a great armed camp — armed alike for the enforcement of imperial authority over its own citizens, and for the extension of that authority over countries which did not as yet recognize it.

Thus at the beginning of the century stood these two kingdoms over against each other, with their diametrically antagonistic principles. The infant church of Christ: a brotherhood of absolute equals, centred in loyalty to an invisible master, enforced only by the individual conscience. The giant empire of Rome: an armed camp, under the absolute authority of an enthroned Cæsar, enforced by a standing army, extending throughout its entire territory, and secured through officials who were classified in ranks and orders according to the measure of their authority. The difference between these two empires is strikingly illustrated by their respective capitals. To the pagan, Rome was "The Eternal City;" the Christian looked for a new Jerusalem descending out of heaven from God.

From the very first, these two organizations instinctively recognized in each other a mortal foe. The Roman empire was tolerant of all religions except the Christian religion; [1] that religion Rome bent all its energies to destroy. The Christian church saw in Rome the incarnation of the world power, and John, the great prophet of the infant church, in a vision beheld the Christ going forth conquering and to conquer until the kingdoms of the world had become the kingdoms of the Lord and of his Christ. The history of the church down to the period of the Reformation is the history of the way in which Christian principles and the Christian spirit pervaded and transformed pagan institutions, and in which Christian institutions were moulded and pervaded by pagan principles. The result in the Middle Ages was an empire partially christianized, and a church partially paganized.

Eulogy and condemnation of the church of the Middle Ages are alike easy; a discriminating judgment is always difficult. The admirers of the papal church — the most splendid, the most enduring, and historically the most powerful of all human organizations — have abundant material for their eulogies. They can point to a life so long that by the side of it the most ancient

[1] It never antagonized the Jewish religion until Christianity issued from Judaism.

Protestant sect is but a youth in its teens; they can point to a missionary zeal so great that by the side of it the greatest missionary triumphs of our Protestant religion, if triumphs are to be measured by majorities, are insignificant. They can point to a self-sacrifice so deep, so abiding, so sacred, that the unbelieving world wonders and the believing world worships, — women denying themselves the sacred joys of wifely and maternal love; men cutting themselves off from the possibility of a home, that they may serve the church, to them wife, mother, father, husband, God. There is no desert where the soldiers of this church have not penetrated, there is no danger which has daunted them, no martyrdom which they have not courted. They have planted the cross in the snows of Kamschatka, and in the burning deserts of Arabia; their missionaries have penetrated without protection other than that of a sincere, enthusiastic, perhaps a fanatical faith, the wilds of China and of Africa, the cities of pagan India and the snow-covered forests of our own North America. Avarice and ambition have had no more devoted adherents than the Church of Rome has had. Seeking for the souls of the Indians, they dared every danger and suffered every privation that the boldest trapper dared or endured. Pestilence has not kept them from the hospital, nor

the bullet from the battle-field. The Church of
Rome has in her true sainthood enrolled the
names of a hundred Howards and Florence
Nightingales.

We read this page in her history with admi-
ration. It is written in letters of living light,
of more than golden glory. We turn the page;
we find on the reverse side a history that fills us
with alternate amazement and indignation — a
history written in letters of blood and of fire.
The cruelties of the Mohammedan Saladin pale
beside those of the Christian Duke of Alva.
Looking into the uncovered dungeons of the Inquisition, no wonder if we forget the patient, un-
tiring self-devotion of the monks of St. Bernard.
The festivities of cruelty that make us turn away
from the pages of Waldensian history blot from
our recollections the undying love of the Jesuit
missionaries in North America. The solemn
tolling of a bell breaks the silence of the midnight, calling to more horrible sacrifices than
ever Phœnician offered to his Moloch, or Druid
to his God. Thirty thousand lives fall in the
Massacre of St. Bartholomew, victims to the
remorseless religious cruelty of this enigmatic
church. For it is in very truth the unsolved
enigma of history, — its flag red on one side
with blood of martyrs whom it has slain, on the
other side red with its own martyrs who have

died for it; bearing the uplifted sword in the one hand, and the uplifted cross in the other; distinguished alike by the names of Loyola and of Xavier, of Torquemada and of Bishop Féne-lon. Enigma as it is, yet he who recognizes that the church is itself an evolution, in which the religious life has struggled for existence and has survived only by proving its right to survival, will find in the doctrine of evolution the explanation of this enigma. The glory of the Roman Catholic Church, the glory of self-sacrifice, is the glory of Christianity; its shame of pride, sensuality, and cruelty is the shame of paganism.

After Christ's death, as the Messiah's expected return was delayed, and the church realized the necessity of a permanent work of preparation for his coming, it realized also the imperative necessity for a permanent organization of his church. They who met at first in private houses for prayer, praise, and mutual instruction very soon began to plan and push forward enterprises for imparting to others the life of faith and hope and love which they themselves possessed. The Jewish law had laid upon the church a duty of charity, and the spirit of Christ converted this duty into an enthusiasm. The forces first of Judaism and then of paganism were alert and aggressive to destroy the infant church, and persecution compelled mutual coöperation for mutual protection. Thus missionary zeal, the enthusiasm of love, and the necessities of self‑defense compelled organization. The early Christian societies were modeled after those of existing institutions. "With probably no single exception," says Professor Hatch, "the names of Christian institutions and Christian officers are shared by them in common with institutions and officers outside of Christianity." Each separate household of faith came to have a presiding officer, sometimes called elder or presbyter, sometimes called overseer or bishop. Then two or more of these households of faith in any given town were united under one president. Then the households of a province were similarly united under a president who himself presided over the work of the other local presidents; and so gradually grew up a systematic and highly organized episcopal system.

By the fourth century the Christian church had become so strong that the sagacious Constantine thought it wiser and easier to use than to fight it. He discovered that "the Christian soldiers were stronger and braver than their fellows," and "man for man and battalion for battalion were more than a match for the pagans." By an imperial decree he made Christianity the religion of the state. But it was the fundamental maxim of the Roman constitution that the care of religion was the right as well as the duty of the civil magistrate. Thus, the decree which made Christianity the religion of the state made Constantine the head of the church. Thus, the conversion of the empire was the perversion of the church. If the one was half Christianized, the other was at the same time and by the same act half paganized. Imperial Christianity was a mongrel religion. Its character is indicated by a single significant fact: the coin which Constantine issued bore the name of Christ on one side, and the figure of Apollo on the other.

As the church waxed stronger and the empire grew weaker, the central and imperial authority was gradually transferred from the Emperor to the Bishop of Rome. It is needless here to trace the process of the transfer. It was effectually symbolized when, A. D. 800, Charlemagne knelt before the high altar of the stateliest temple of Christian Rome, and received from the hands of the Pope the diadem of the Cæsars. From that day the Church of Rome has maintained with an obstinate consistency that it is the right of the Pope, as the Vicar of God, to give the crown to whom he will, and take it away when the king proves himself unworthy. True, the Popes have not always been successful in maintaining this authority. Sometimes the Emperor has been subject to the Pope, sometimes the Pope has been subject to the Emperor, and sometimes the two have shared the authority between them. But the claim to imperial authority asserted by Leo III. in the coronation of Charlemagne has never been formally withdrawn or disavowed by any successor, from that day to this.

With this adoption of the imperialism of Rome by the church of Christ, there came necessarily the adoption of its bureaucratic method. It is impossible for the head of a paternal government to exercise his authority directly over all his subjects, as the father of a family may over his children. That authority must be entrusted to subordinates and transmitted through them. Thus grew up in the church of Rome a hierarchy whose offices were analogous to those of the Roman empire, and whose very names, as we have seen, were borrowed from their pagan prototypes. Father, Rabbi, Master, whom Christ had said should not exist in his church, were all transferred with imperialism from pagan to papal Rome. And this transmutation of the Christian into the pagan organization was necessarily followed by the repudiation of Christ's principle that force was not to be employed in his church.

In pagan thought the Christian idea of punishment as remedial found absolutely no place.

The object of pagan punishment was either the gratification of a personal revenge, the exercise of what is called vindictive justice, or the deterring of other criminals from the perpetration of similar crimes. With these three objects in view, the punishments were made as cruel as possible. This pagan conception of punishment has not even in our day been wholly eliminated, and we are only very gradually learning that mercy has more power than cruelty to deter. In the Middle Ages, the punishments inflicted by the state were pitiless. "The wheel, the cauldron of boiling oil, burning alive, burying alive, flaying alive, tearing apart with wild horses, were the ordinary expedients by which the criminal jurist sought to deter crime by frightful examples which would make a profound impression on a not over-sensitive population."[1] In England, theft was punished by burning; in France, by burying alive; in Germany, murder and arson were punished by breaking on the wheel. In Denmark, blasphemers first had their tongues cut out and then were beheaded. In Hanover, the false coiner was punished by being burned to death. When the church once adopted the principle that force might be used for the punishment of heresy, it was inevita-

[1] H. C. Lea's *History of the Inquisition*, vol. i. 234, from which also the other illustrations are taken.

ble that it should use the cruel punishments in vogue in its own age. Yet it adopted this principle only gradually and reluctantly. The first persecutions for religious opinion were introduced by Constantine, and against them bishops in the church vigorously protested. The first persecuting bishops were compelled to resign. Even as late as the eleventh century, persecution of heretics by the church was compelled by the mob in spite of ineffectual resistance by the ecclesiastics. The truth that no opinion, however erroneous, can be a sin, is still unrecognized by the majority of the church.[1] It is not strange that in the Middle Ages such false opinions were regarded as crimes; and as injuries to the soul are greater than injuries to the body, and as apostasy from God is a greater sin than treason to the state, it is not strange that no punishment was deemed too severe for these, the greatest and the most pernicious crimes.

Thus, by the fifteenth century the abandonment of Christ's principles seemed to be complete. The bond which united the church was not loyalty to Christ, but loyalty to the Bishop of Rome. The Christian brotherhood was abandoned, and for it was substituted an elabo-

---

[1] I assume, without discussion, that sin consists in the act of the will, and therefore that no purely intellectual act can be sinful, though it may grow out of sin or lead into sin.

rate ecclesiastical hierarchy. The principle that the only force to be used in the church is that of the individual conscience had given place to the use of the rack, the fagot, and the sword. The medal given by Gregory VII. to the Knights of St. John, having the cross on one side and the sword on the other, was a true sample of the adoption by the church of the military methods of the pagan empire. The very word "spiritual" had lost its signification. Ecclesiastics, if they were duly ordained; buildings, if they were properly consecrated; and even lands, if they belonged to the church, had become "spiritual."

A beautiful legend of this epoch illustrates the change which had passed over the spirit of the church. According to this legend, Jesus Christ comes back upon the earth, and shows himself at a great *auto da fé* in Seville, where hundreds of heretics are burned in his honor. He walks about in the ashes of the martyrs. The common people throng about him, and he blesses them. The chief Inquisitor causes him to be arrested and at midnight visits him in his cell. "You are wrong," says the Inquisitor, "in coming again to the earth to interfere in the work of your church. You were wrong not to accept the offer of the Tempter, wrong to undertake to convert the world by silent and spiritual forces.

There are but three forces on earth which can keep humanity in check, — the miracle, the mystery, and the authority. You have rejected them all, to proclaim a freedom and a love for which mankind are not ready. It has been necessary for the church to correct your work and supplement it with the sword of Cæsar. You also, to-morrow, shall be burned, for you shall not be permitted to interfere with the work of your church." Christ answers not a word, looks into the eyes of the Inquisitor with mild, familiar gaze, then stoops and kisses the old man on his bloodless mouth. The old man trembles, opens the cell door, and bids the Master depart, never to return. Eloquently does the legend indicate the change which had come over the spirit of Christ's church since the days of Christ.

And yet, if Christianity had been corrupted by paganism, paganism had been ameliorated by Christianity. The Roman Catholic Church was not exceptionally cruel; it shared the cruelty of a cruel age. Really denying, it in form recognized Christ's fundamental principle, that force is not to be used in the maintenance of his kingdom. It did not itself punish heresy. It tried and condemned the heretic, and then turned him over to the civil authorities to be punished for the crime of which he was convicted. If the state refused to punish crime and maintain order and truth, the church absolved the citizens from their allegiance to the king on the ground that the king had failed of his solemn duty. If like Frederick II. of Germany, the king was an infidel, or like John of England, an apostate, the church claimed the right to dethrone him and put another and a loyal king in his place. But the punishments inflicted for heresy were inflicted in the name of the state, to whose mercy the church in terms always commended the heretic.

The Roman Catholic bureaucracy, unlike that of imperial Rome, was a democratic bureaucracy. The humblest person might, and sometimes did become Pope, and he earned that office by services rendered, not always indeed to humanity, but always to the church. The brotherhood which Christ had sketched existed in fragmentary and modified forms in various monastic orders. The Latin tongue was adopted as the language of the church under all skies and in all nations. The church, by preaching the unity of God, laid the foundation for a true unity of Christendom. The confederation of the churches throughout the Roman empire created a common life. Poverty in one section was felt as a common sorrow, and was alleviated by contributions from the churches far and near.

The foundation of a public opinion was laid in a system of instruction, which, emanating from and ruled over by one head, was essentially one, and by a spiritual life which, though corrupted by gross superstitions, bound the church together. The Pope was without any considerable army. His only force was this public opinion which the church had created and kept alive. It was before this public opinion that kings trembled and bowed. It was to this public opinion that finally the church itself was compelled to bow.

Though the Bishop of Rome took the place of the Emperor of Rome, and though allegiance to him, not to the invisible Christ, became the bond of union of the church, still the emperor was not deified. He was not God, but the Vicar of God. Households raised no altars to his name; no church worshiped him; and when at St. Peter's the Host, symbol of Christ, was raised in air, Pope, cardinal, bishop, priest, altar boy, and peasant bowed together in reverence before it.

The Reformation was primarily the protest of the Teutonic race against the imperialism of Rome. The doctrine that every man shall give account of himself to God was Luther's war-cry, and it became the central doctrine of Calvinism. The early Reformers did not see the

full significance of this doctrine, but it necessarily carries with it the abolition of the use
of force in the church. The last remnant of
Roman militarism lingers in the ecclesiastical
trials of our day, whose only penalty upon the
offending clergyman is a new ecclesiastical affi-
liation, with usually a larger congregation and
a greater influence and prestige than before.
Protestantism, abandoning the doctrine of force,
abandoned also the Roman emperor as the centre ·of the church, and loyalty to the Roman
emperor as its bond of union. But it did not
make Jesus Christ, as a personal and living
Master, its centre, nor has it been content to
make simple loyalty to him the only condition
of membership and the only bond of union. In
lieu thereof it offers three substitutes. The Reformed churches propose a creed; they recur
from Roman imperialism to Greek philosophy;
the church, from being an army, becomes a
school of philosophy. The Anglicans affirm an
apostolical succession; they recur to Judaism;
and propose, as the bond uniting their churches
in an organism, a spiritualized survival of the
Aaronic priesthood. Finally, the Independents
abolish church unity altogether; and for a planetary system substitute a universe of wandering
comets. Thus in the Protestant church of to-
day the use of force as a means of maintaining

authority is abandoned, though there is not yet a frank recognition of the supreme authority of conscience ; and offices are coming to be places of service, not of authority, though the distinction between the two functions is not sharply drawn. But the problem of church unity remains still unsolved. The church of to-day is still a composite. In it, more than in any other organization, is the spirit of faith and hope and love manifested. Its life is the life of Christ, but its organization is still pagan, Jewish, or a composite of the two. The organization of the church of Rome is a survival of Cæsarism; that of Anglicanism is a survival of Judaism; that of the Reformed or Presbyterian churches is a survival of Greek schools of philosophy; and that of the Independents or Congregationalists is a survival of Teutonic individualism.

What of the future? How shall the unsolved problem of church unity be solved? Not by going back to papal imperialism. There is, indeed, no danger to American civilization in the papal church. The Inquisition will never be revived. It belonged not to the church, but to a barbarism which Christianity has already conquered. But the papal church is neither our model nor our goal. It is a strange amalgam. Its bloodless sacrifice of the Mass, its Eternal

City, its Pope and priesthood, are relics of the sacrificial and hierarchical system of Judaism. Its mediatorial theology, its intercession of saints and angels, its adoration of images, and its absolutism in government are relics of Roman paganism. Its monasteries and convents are curious specimens of the arrested development of that brotherhood of man which has found in our later days larger, better, and more Christian expression. Its confessional for private counsel, its absolution, giving public and authoritative declaration of the forgiveness of sins, and its self-sacrificing spirit, shown in many a monk, missionary, and priest, all manifest, though in forms somewhat archaic, the spirit of the gospel, and furnish both inspiration and suggestion to those who deny the authority of the Church of Rome, and find no help to their spiritual life in its Jewish and Roman symbolism. Take it for all in all, the Christian evolutionist sees in the Church of Rome, not an antichrist, but a specimen of arrested Christian development, the remedy for which is not war, but education, not theological polemics, but the schoolhouse.

Nor will church unity be secured by accepting, as the final word of God's Providence, Presbyterianism. The creed is not the centre of the church, loyalty to the creed is not the bond of union. The intellect is divisive. Creeds are not intended to unite men, but to separate them. From the Nicene Creed down to the last creed of Congregationalism, there is not one which had not for its prime object the exclusion of certain classes of men from the organization which adopted the creed as its platform. The Nicene Creed was framed to exclude the Arians; the Decrees of the Council of Trent were framed to exclude Protestants; the Westminster Confession of Faith was framed to exclude Arminians; the Episcopal Thirty-nine Articles were framed to exclude Roman Catholics and Independents; and the latest creed of Congregationalism was framed to exclude Unitarians and Universalists. The church which adopts a creed as its centre, and loyalty to a creed as its bond of union, is a school of philosophy. Its assumed function is to teach a system, not to proclaim a person.

Nor does Episcopacy answer the unanswered problem of church unity. The bishops of the Episcopal Church propose four conditions of Christian union, the Bible, the Nicene Creed, the two sacraments, and the historic Episcopacy. The first two conditions are Protestant, a revival of Greek philosophy; the second two conditions are Roman and Jewish, a revival of a semi-imperial hierarchy. But the church is a circle, not an ellipse; with one centre, not with two foci.

That centre is loyalty to Christ alone. It is not loyalty to a Book, though the book gives us information concerning the Christ; it is not loyalty to a creed, though the creed may admirably express the opinion of a noble age concerning the Christ; it is not loyalty to an organization or hierarchy, though that organization or hierarchy may be admirably adapted to do the work of the Christ; and it is not loyalty to ceremonials, few or many, though they may be splendid and useful symbols of the spiritual life.

Nor are we to abandon the problem of church unity altogether, and substitute for the church of Christ an aggregation of individual and independent assemblies. If the papacy is a survival of Roman imperialism, Presbyterianism of Greek philosophical schools, and Episcopacy of a Judaic hierarchy, Independency is a survival of Teutonic individualism; as essentially incongruous with the ideal toward which all churches should set their face as are either of its sister systems. The church of Christ, as Christ and the Apostles depicted it, is an organic thing, with a unity, an organic life, a historical continuity. When the Apostle declares that the church is the bride of the Lamb, it is not a Solomon's harem he has in mind. When he declares that the church is the body in which God tabernacles, he is not thinking of a number of *dis-*

jecta membra. The river of God is not meant to separate into multitudinous streams as it nears the sea, like the Nile at the Delta. We do not all come unto the unity of the faith and of the knowledge of the Son of God, unto a perfect man in Christ Jesus, by splitting up into warring sects with polemical creeds and pugilistic piety. The glory of God in his church is not best seen by breaking it up into bits, each with its own peculiar shape and peculiar color, tumbled promiscuously together and showing a new pattern with every turn of the kaleidoscope. The church described in the New Testament is a tree, rooted and grounded in Christ; a body, Christ the head; a household, Christ the father; a kingdom, Christ the king. The true church of Christ is one; but the unity of the church lies in the future. We shall not come to it until we recognize that loyalty to Christ — the historic Christ, the risen and living Christ — is the sole condition of union, and in that union is absolute liberty of thought, of worship, and of action. Christ the only Pope, Christ the only creed, they who possess Christ's spirit the only apostolical succession; and all who are in Christ one, because they are in him, and are doing his work.

CHAPTER VI.

THE EVOLUTION OF CHRISTIAN SOCIETY.

THE first century of the Christian era was morally the darkest in history. The apparent splendor of the Roman Empire did not conceal from even its own thinkers the corruption which foretold approaching dissolution. The moral influences of the past seemed to have spent themselves, and no new power of righteousness had arisen for Rome's redemption. Government was an absolute despotism. Society was divided into two classes — many paupers and a few rich. Public corruption was not a public disgrace. Gluttony and drunkenness were fine arts, and licentiousness and prostitution a religion. The laborers were slaves; public education there was none; marriage was a partnership dissoluble at the will of either partner. In Palestine, also, there was decay, though yet not so complete. Thanks to the system of public education which Moses had founded, there was a parochial school for the children of the peasantry in every village that had a synagogue; thanks to the restrictions which Moses had put about slavery and polygamy, there were few or no slaves in Jewish households, and not a harem in all Palestine. And yet even in Palestine the church had fallen under the dominion of a corrupt and infidel priesthood, who were agnostics in their creed, though they were still ritualists in their practice.

At this time there appeared a young man of thirty whose brief life and simple teaching were to reconstruct the social order. He never went beyond the bounds of his own little province. He gathered a few hundred of the common peasantry about him, and talked to them of truth, duty, love, God. He told them that the world was not orphaned ; that it had a Father in heaven who loved his children, cared for them, suffered with them. He told them that all men were brethren ; that distinctions between rich and poor, high and low, cultured and ignorant, between Hebrew and Greek, between Jew and pagan, — differences of ritual, of creed, of condition, of race, — were of small consequence; that the only vital distinction was between righteousness and unrighteousness, truth and falsehood, virtue and vice, love and malice. He told them that life was for service ; that to be useful was to be great; that to be self-denying was to be happy ; that sorrow rightly borne was a blessing, not a bane ; that the way to overcome evil was by love and patience, not by force. Moses had told the Jew to love his Jewish neighbor as himself; Jesus told him that the apostate and heretical Samaritan was his neighbor. Moses had forbidden cruel and disproportionate punishments; only maim, he said, the one that maims; kill only the one who has killed. Christ went further. Do not punish sin at all, he said; cure it. Love is better than justice; a penitentiary than a prison; a reformatory than a jail. Resist not evil; do good to them that despitefully use you. Moses had told them that God was justice — too holy to clear the guilty; Jesus told them that God was love — so holy that he would cure the guilty. He came as a physician to cure the sin-sick. Forgiveness of sin, deliverance from sin, was his mission. He told them that not ignorance, nor wretchedness, nor race, nor even sin separated the soul from God. The more the soul needed God, the readier was God to give the help of his companionship.

He, however, made no attempt to reform the institutions of society. He declared that marriage was not a commercial partnership, but a divinely ordained and ordered life, and he condemned free divorce; but with this exception he uttered no explicit directions respecting civil or political institutions. As he prescribed no ritual, creed, or ecclesiastical organization, so he framed no civic order. He uttered no counsels respecting forms of government, and one cannot deduce from his teaching whether he approved of monarchy, aristocracy, oligarchy, or democracy. He said nothing respecting slavery, the industrial organization which was then almost universally prevalent. He made no attempt to institute any system of public education or to improve the schools which in Palestine were connected with the Jewish synagogues. It has been said that Jesus Christ was the first socialist. This is certainly an incorrect, if not an absolutely erroneous statement. It would be more nearly correct to say that he was the first individualist. The socialist assumes that the prolific cause of misery in the world is bad social organization, and that the first duty of the philanthropist is to reform social organizations. Christ assumed that the prolific cause of misery in the world is individual wrong doing, and he set himself to the work of curing the individual. He was not a reformer, he was a life-giver, and giving life he left it to form its own social as its own religious organizations. But he taught both implicitly and explicitly that the effect of the life which he gave would be to change radically the social organizations of the world. His first preaching was as a herald proclaiming that the kingdom of God was at hand. His first great sermon, the only one which has been preserved to us in anything like completeness, was an exposition of the principles which would underlie and the spirit which would pervade this kingdom. And the disciple who stood nearest to him, and understood him best, declared in the later years of his life, his faith in the social and civic character of Christianity by the assertion that the kingdoms of this world would become the kingdom of our Lord and of his Christ.

In order to understand the nature of the life which Jesus Christ imparted, we must take into account the Jewish religion, upon which, as on a foundation, he based his own instructions. We must remember that Judaism and Christianity are the same religion, one in the bud, the other in the blossom. Faith in man is as characteristic of this religion as faith in God. According to its teaching, the whole human race descends from one pair and have one blood. The kinship which unites men in one great brotherhood is more fundamental and more enduring than that which unites them in separate tribes, nations, or races. Man, not a particular class or clan of men, is made in God's image. To man it is given to exercise dominion over all nature. Sin is a fault not natural, but distinctly and emphatically unnatural, contra-natural, against man's true, real nature. The theology of Judaism is based on the fundamental doctrine that man is of kin to God. The religious appeals of the prophets are to man's inherent and indestructible divine nature. The civic institutions of Judaism are based on the same fundamental assumption, — man's inherent capability to solve the problems of his own destiny under the immediate guidance and direction of God. When the Jewish commonwealth was to be founded, the assent of the people was first secured. Not even God would assume to be their king until they had by popular suffrage accepted him.[1] The officers of the commonwealth were similarly elected by popular, if not by universal suffrage, and were responsible to the people who had elected them. The problems of the national life were discussed and determined by two representative bodies, a Great Congregation, answering to our House of Representatives, and a Council of Elders, answering to our Senate. Local self-government was provided for by the organization of the nation into twelve tribes, each with its separate territory. Government was divided into three great departments, the legislative, the executive, and the judicial ; a division which experience has since demonstrated

[1] Exodus xix. 3–8.

to be essential to the continuance of freedom. The adjustment of penalty to transgression was not left to the discretion of judges, nor to that of an imperial despot, but was determined by explicit and definite statutes. Neither landed gentry nor hereditary caste was allowed in this commonwealth. A priesthood was organized, but it was forbidden any share in the distribution of the land, and was made dependent on the voluntary contributions of the people. Agriculture was encouraged, war was discouraged; slavery and polygamy were hedged about with such restrictions that they both ceased to exist; the education of the common people was provided for, at first by itinerant prophets and Levites, later by parochial schools connected with the synagogues; and when finally the republic became a monarchy, the appointment of a king was permitted only as a concession to public prejudice.[1]

To a people thus prepared by a conception of human dignity unparalleled elsewhere among the nations of the earth, comes the Christ. His coming gives to all that believe in him a new sense of the value and the dignity of mankind. Whatever our estimate of Christ may be, the

[1] A fuller exposition of the practical principles of the Hebraic commonwealth will be found in my *Jesus of Nazareth*, chap. ii.

estimate of the Apostolic church is not doubtful.   Matthew saw in him the Messiah, the Son
of the Living God ; John beheld him the Word
of God made flesh and tabernacling among us.
Paul bowed the knee to him as one who, being
in the form of God, beggared himself that he
might be made in the form of a servant; the
unknown author of the Epistle to the Hebrews
believed him to be the creator of the world, the
brightness of God's glory, and the express image
of his person.   Put what philosophical interpretation we may upon their expressions of primitive faith, we cannot doubt that those who uttered them saw in this coming of God into a
human life a new glorification of humanity.
The Roman, by deifying man had degraded the
conception of God ; the Christian, by humaniz-
ing God had glorified the conception of man.
For God had chosen man to be his tabernacle,
his dwelling place, his image, the medium for
his manifestation of himself.

Entering humanity, God entered into one
of the humblest class.   It was not priest or
king, but peasant child, whom he chose for his
indwelling.   So entering life, he addressed himself to the lowest and the outcast.   He recognized a divinity in every man, and spake that
he might evoke and inspire that divinity.   Himself a peasant in his youth, he gathered his im-

mediate disciples from the peasant class. The nascent Christianity caught this spirit of its founder and entered the Roman Empire at the bottom. It passed by the rich and the noble, it gathered its recruits from the freedmen and the slaves. The message of the Christian religion to a people living in hopelessness was one of inspiration. You are, it said to them, the children of God; you have before you an immortal destiny; the world's deliverer, who is yet to be crowned Lord of lords and King of kings, is one of your own class, a peasant like yourself; God has entered him that he may enter you, and in him has glorified the humblest and the lowest. Human hearts responded to this trumpet-call of hope. Self-respect and with it mutual respect were aroused in the hearts of a class which had hitherto known only universal contempt. The history of the first four centuries of the Christian church is, politically speaking, the history of a great popular uprising, the cause of which was the awakening of a profound and inspiring religious life. When in the fourth century Constantine yielded and made Christianity the religion of the state, it was to a new-born democracy he yielded; it was a new-born democracy he summoned to be his ally.

In all subsequent history the power of the Roman church was the power of the common peo-

ple. The Popes, in the epoch when their dominion was least questioned, possessed no army of
any consequence. They appealed to the people,
and by their appeals to the people they ruled
over kings. It was democracy which in the person of Leo III. crowned Charlemagne, and later
in the person of Gregory VII. kept the Emperor
of Germany shivering in a penitent's shirt, waiting permission to enter the pontiff's presence.
The Reformation was a further uprising of a
more enlightened and a more free-spirited people. It was Teuton versus Roman. Almost
the sole power of Luther in his battle with
Rome was the power of a public opinion which
Rome could neither suppress nor control. It
was public opinion which enabled Henry VIII.
to emancipate England from the political power
of the Pope; which checked Bloody Mary in her
sanguinary course; pushed on Queen Elizabeth
to a larger and more radical reformation than
she ever intended or desired; dethroned and
beheaded Charles I., and dethroned and exiled
James II.; and has by successive revolutions,
some of them peaceful and others warlike, com-
pletely changed the character, while preserving
the form, of the British Constitution.

This public opinion created by Christianity,
organized and solidified unconsciously by the
Roman Catholic Church, inspired with a new

spirit by the Teutonic incursion, and at once creating and re-created by Protestantism, laid here on this continent, in a Christian faith, the foundation of a new form of government. The Puritans in New England, the Dutch in New York, the Roman Catholics in Maryland, the Anglicans in Virginia, and the Huguenots in France, widely as they differed from one another in their denominational tenets, possessed a common faith in God as the All Father, and in man as his child. They derived from a common source — the Jewish and the Christian Scriptures — that faith in the capacity of man without which free institutions are impossible.

They thus prepared this country for that government by public opinion which is the essence of a true democracy. Jefferson is reputed to have said that if he had to choose between a country with newspapers and without government, and a country with government and without newspapers, he would choose the former. To say that Americans have chosen the former would be to sacrifice truth to antithesis; but they have developed a life in which newspapers make and unmake governments. The newspaper is the voice of public opinion, and it is this fact which gives the press its power. The voice is sometimes coarse, sometimes immoral, oftener unmoral; but it faithfully repeats the sentiments of its constituency. The newspaper brings the community to a consciousness of its own inner life. Each separate journal reflects by its advertisements the trade, by its news columns the conduct, by its editorials the thoughts and feelings, of the world whose organ it is. And every newspaper is an organ of some constituency. Whenever it breaks away from its constituency and misrepresents its readers, it loses its power and prestige, as more than one instance in the history of American journalism demonstrates. To thoughtful men the condition of American journalism is far from satisfactory; the press of to-day is more enterprising than educative; and there seems to be even a decadence, moral and intellectual, since the days of Greeley, Raymond, Bryant, and Bowles. But to the student of our national life the reason is plain. Our public schools have taught great masses of men to read who have not yet learned to think; and our more widely circulated, not necessarily our more influential journals, represent a reading, but not a thoughtful constituency. It is on the whole an advantage to have life photographed; it is well that half the world should know how the other half lives; and the evolutionist looks with hope for the day when a better education will correct the evils of an imperfect education, and the press will improve because the public whose voice it is has improved.

Meanwhile we can hardly fail to see, whether the fact inspires satisfaction or regret, that the press is really more potent than legislatures. To vacate one of the more influential editorial chairs for a seat in Congress is a distinct descent from a position of larger to one of lesser influence. The press in reflecting helps also to shape public opinion, which in turn creates legislatures and coerces them to do its bidding. Our lawmakers no longer really govern, nor even discuss problems of government; they only embody in legal forms the decisions to which the community has come, by discussion in public assemblages and through the public press. Every interest has today its journal, and almost every interest its Congress. A Prison Congress outlines and demands prison reform; a Banking Association formulates the principles of banking and currency to be incorporated in state and national legislation; a Lake Mohonk Conference shapes the course of the nation towards the Indians; a Civil Service Reform Association secures reform as fast as it is able to create a public opinion favorable to reform; a Liquor Dealers Association demands less restraint, and various temperance and Christian bodies demand more restraint, on the liquor traffic, and legislation oscillates between the two, almost exactly registering the state of public opinion in each local community. Thus for a government of the one over the all (monarchy) and government of the few over the many (oligarchy) has been substituted that self-government, through the power of a public opinion, which gives, not indeed always the best immediate government, but always the freest, the most progressive, and the most hopeful for the future. It is needless to trace in further detail the progress of this development. Enough has been said in this rapid survey to show that Christianity is the source of that uprising in the individual without which the uprising of the mass would have been impossible. All good government is aristocratic, that is, the government of the best over the inferior. Various attempts have been made in the world's history to select the best class to rule over the inferior classes. Christianity evokes the best in each individual to rule over his inferior self, and thus lays the foundation for self-government in the community by making possible self-government in the individual.

If the reader believes this rapid survey of the political history of Europe to be correct, he will readily see that Christianity, in creating government by public opinion, has with it created great political and social changes. It is not possible within the limits of a single chapter to trace these changes in detail, nor is it necessary. It is sufficient to indicate very briefly some of the more important of them. He who is interested in tracing them out more fully will find the material in such works as Charles L. Brace's "Gestæ Christi," Dr. R. S. Storrs' "Historical Evidences of Christianity," and Lecky's "History of Christian Morals."

I. Government has passed through one radical change, but only to enter upon another which may possibly prove to be not less radical. The earliest government was that of the family; and the earliest tribal and national governments were formed upon the pattern of the family. The king, as father of his nation, ruled over it. He was thought to be endowed with a supernatural grace and wisdom; and his people were regarded as children, quite unable to care for themselves. Christianity has already proved to the German race, and is convincing the Latin races, that men are men, not children, and do not need a political father to take care of them. Under this tuition the first step is to take from the king his paternal authority, to organize the state upon the principle of the sovereignty of the people, and to reduce government to the minimum necessary in order to protect the community from wrong-doing at the hands of other communities, and the individual in the community from wrong-doing at the hands of other individuals.

But already men are beginning to question whether, if the individual can take care of himself without paternal interference, the community cannot by common action take care of its common interests. Undoubtedly it requires a much higher degree of intellectual and moral development for fifty million people to coöperate in industrial partnership, than it does for any individual to act alone, or in coöperation with a few like-minded with himself. Socialism affirms that men possess this higher intellectual and moral capacity; or if this is not yet their possession, that it is within their reach. Thus, under the influence of Christianity, with its optimistic faith in man, — a faith quite incredible except as it is founded upon a faith in God the All-Father, — government is undergoing a transition through three successive stages, which may be expressed by the words, Paternalism, Individualism, Fraternalism. Even the ultra-socialist is not, what he is sometimes called, a paternalist. He is a fraternalist. His schemes are founded on his belief, not in the incapacity, but in the capacity of man. He does not propose that a paternal government shall do for him, but that by communal action he shall do for himself. Bossism has been driven from the church; is being driven from the state; and the socialist hopes that it will be driven from the mine and the factory. What progress has been made in free commonwealths in this direction is hardly realized by most men, so rapidly and yet so silently have the changes been wrought. It is less than a century since the question was seriously discussed whether letters could not be more advantageously carried by private enterprise than by government. Now, in England, the telegraph is a branch of the post-office; in Switzerland all express business is conducted by the government; in Australia all railroads are owned and operated by the government; while city after city, both in this country and abroad, has initiated municipal industries, including governmental ownership and control of water supply, lighting, and transportation. I make no mention of the progress in this direction in Germany, where both banking and insurance have become distinctly governmental functions, since it may be a fair question whether in Germany these are the products of a paternal or a fraternal government. But on the other hand, the student of modern history should not overlook the fact that by far the greatest proportion of the educational work of this country is carried on under the immediate direction of the people themselves, and this in every grade from the kindergarten to the university, and even to the post-graduate and professional school.

This movement toward fraternalism in government is still in its experimental stage, and so far as the wisdom of these experiments depends on the question of the proper function of government, it is one about which Christianity has nothing to say. It may well be that as church and state are better separated, so are church and industry. It may well be that the organization which governs would better not be the organization which carries on great industrial enterprises, even those which are of a common concern. It would be foreign to my purpose to enter upon that question here. It must suffice to say that the Christian evolutionist will, if he is consistent, base his objection to state control or even to state ownership of railroads, mines, telegraphs, banks, and other common enterprises, on some other ground than the absolute and ineradicable incapacity of the common people to control or even to conduct them.[1]

[1] That I may not seem to my reader to come perilously near a debated question only skillfully to evade it, I may add that according to my judgment industrial and political functions are different; that any movement for enlarging the functions of government in the direction of industrial enterprises should be very cautious; but that I believe — subject

II. The relation of Christianity to science may not be at first very evident; for the Bible contains no revelation of any scientific truths; the indications are that its writers shared the scientific opinions of their age; and if Christ himself knew better about the laws of nature than did his contemporaries, it is certain that he did nothing to enlighten them on that subject. No important additions to the scientific knowledge of the race can, so far as I know, be attributed to the early Hebrew people. But the scientific development which characterizes this age would have been impossible had it not been for the inculcation of two moral principles by the Bible, to both of which I have already referred.

The first is the Biblical teaching that nature is subject to the dominion of men; rather the profounder teaching that the physical is wholly subject to the dominion of the spiritual. Nature is depersonified in the first chapter of Genesis, and

to a change of mind as the result of actual experiment — that the people have the right to conduct any public industrial enterprises, the conduct of which is essential to their common well being, such as street lighting, transportation, water supply, and the like, which upon actual experiment it appears they can conduct more economically and efficiently for themselves, through public officials, than by entrusting them to private enterprise and paying " what the business will bear."

never in the history of the Jews are there traces of that personification which is almost universal in other lands. We meet in Hebrew literature with no sprites, or nymphs, or fauns, or gnomes, or fairies, or Robin Goodfellows. God is immanent in nature ; and man as the son of God shares God's mastery and dominion over nature. So long as men believed that the lightning was the thunderbolt of Jove, it was impossible that they should attempt to catch it and send it on their errands. The faith that all material things are subject to a spiritual lordship is essential to scientific exploration, much more to scientific dominion over nature.

Nor are the teachings and spirit of Christianity less a prerequisite to all that phase of scientific development which has for its inspiration a sense of public welfare. A community which existed only for a small wealthy class could not have invented the press, the power loom, the photograph, the railroad, the steamboat, and the telegraph. The secret of these great inventions has been the uprising of the people, and their demand for greater facilities and a larger life. Thus faith which sees the superiority of the invisible to the visible, and love which seeks the greatest good of the greatest number, have been necessary partners in the scientific development of the race ; and that scientific development has been therefore not only confined to Christendom, but chiefly to those regions and those epochs in which Christian life and spirit have been most pervasive.

III. It can hardly be necessary to point out the very apparent fact that popular education and Christianity have been both contemporaneous and geographically co-terminous; for the schools of China cannot be said to furnish an education, since they do not teach their pupils to think. In the first century, as I have already pointed out, the only system of popular education in the Roman Empire was that which was organized in connection with the Jewish synagogues, for the children of Jewish parents. Primitive as were the methods employed, we might learn something from them, for these schools furnished both religious and industrial education. As Christianity extended over Europe, it created both a desire for knowledge and the schools to gratify that desire. Every monastery and convent had its library; many of them their schools for the children of the town. That we have to-day any copies of the Bible, or of the Greek and Latin classics, is due to the monastic libraries and the monastic copyists. Modern agriculture dates from the experimental schools of the Benedictine monks. The first seeds of the English revolution were sown by the democratic teaching of the Franciscan friars in the towns and cities of England. When public education had gone so far that it became dangerous to the clergy, the clergy endeavored to halt it. But the mind refuses to stop, let who will cry halt! When ecclesiasticism began to educate men, not for their own sake, but for the sake of the church, democracy took the work of self-education into its own hands. The public school has taken the place of the parochial school. The questions that arise between the two are not those of method merely. The message of the parochial school is, Believe and obey. The message of the public school is, Inquire and act. The one aims to enforce authority, the other to give liberty; the one to build up out of obedient children a great church, the other, out of independent thinkers, a free commonwealth. The school will not again nestle under the rafters of the monastery or the church; but it should not dishonorably forget its parentage because it has grown strong enough to live alone.

IV. The change in criminal law wrought by Christianity is equally plain, and may be indicated in as few words. The punishments of paganism were at first acts of personal vengeance. The next of kin was left to avenge the murder of his relations. Public offenses against the state were personal wrongs against the king, and in the punishments inflicted he embodied the vindictive justice of the state, when he did not gratify his own vindictive passions. How cruel were the punishments which were invented under the inspiration of such a philosophy we have already seen. Christianity declared that it was not the function of men to judge and punish their fellow-men. Judge not, Christ said; vindictive justice does not belong to man. My followers are to remit sin, not to avenge it. The Roman Catholic Church has accepted this mission more fully than has the Protestant Church; and in this fact consists one great element of her spiritual power. But, gradually, in the best penological system we are approximating Christian philosophy. Our prisons are made penitentiaries; our jails reformatories. The most advanced penologists have now nearly arrived at the conclusions announced as premises by Jesus Christ, eighteen centuries ago. The latest and best form of penal administration treats the criminal as it treats the lunatic, — imprisons him, not to inflict vengeance on him for a crime committed, but to cure him of the disposition to commit crime in the future; organizes its punishments, its industries, its schools, with reference to creating a new habit of life and a new nature in the criminal; detains him in prison until the reform is accomplished ; and releases him as soon as satisfactory evidence is afforded that he has both the ability and the steadfast purpose to live henceforth by honorable industry. Thus redemption is substituted for vengeance as the end of punishment. The significance of this revolution is hardly understood even by those who have been promoting it ; still less by the public, who desire only to inflict their vengeance on the criminal, or to get rid of him and forget him altogether. Space does not allow me to trace here the gradual process by which this evolution in criminal jurisprudence has been wrought, and show how to the intervention of the church is due the early engrafting of the principle of mercy on the system of so-called justice, — a principle which is radically changing the original stock. It must suffice to remind the reader that the ecclesiastical system of penances and purgatory was the first organized method of punishment in human society of which the avowed end was not vengeance but reformation ; that the right of sanctuary, the essential idea of which was derived from the old Levitical " cities of refuge," was the first attempt to alleviate the administration of a rude justice by the principle of mercy ; and that courts of equity were created to mitigate the severity of Roman law in order to make the results of jurisprudence accord with the demands of a partially christianized conscience.

V. The same influence which gradually emancipated the state from the despotic control of an irresponsible despot gradually took the shackles off the limbs of the laborer. The Jewish religion honored labor. One of its most ancient traditions represents the first man as placed in a garden to dress and to keep it. The patriarchs, fathers of the race, were men of peaceful industry, not warriors, except as self-protection necessitated war. The greatest king of Israel, David, and her two greatest prophets, Moses and Isaiah, were taken from agricultural pursuits. The nation was bidden by its constitution to depend on a volunteer militia, to allow no standing army. The Messiah whom the Christians proclaimed as the deliverer of the world was born as the son of a carpenter, and had himself worked at the bench. His immediate followers were peasants, who depended for their livelihood on the work of their own hands. This honor paid to toil was carried with Christianity wherever it went. In the opinion of the Christian church, idleness was a disgrace, poverty was not. At the same time the doctrine of human brotherhood was not only preached by the apostles of the new movement, but enforced by the consideration that the time was short in which caste distinctions would be recognized. As the church grew in power, the one distinction between clergy and laity dwarfed all others. Thus while the slave was taught that he was a son of God, the master was taught to treat his slaves as a brother in the household of faith. Christianity and Roman slavery could not co-exist. At first, emancipation was of individuals, then of increasing numbers. "St. Melanie was said to have emancipated 8000 slaves; St. Ovidius, a rich martyr of Gaul, 5000 ; Chromatious, the Roman prefect under Diocletian, 1400 ; Hermes, a prefect in the reign of Trajan, 1250. . . . Numerous charters and epitaphs still record the gift of liberty to slaves throughout the Middle Ages, for the benefit of the soul of the donor or testator. . . . In the twelfth century slaves were very rare. In the fourteenth century slavery was almost unknown." [1] Despite many assertions to the contrary, despite some ground for them in a practical apostasy from Christian principle within the church of Christ, it may be safely affirmed that emancipation in Great Britain and in this country would not have been possible but for the influence of Christianity in awakening and strengthening those sentiments of humanity which finally proved too strong for the political and commercial influ-

[1] Lecky's *History of European Morals*, ii. 73-76.

ences leagued together to perpetuate and extend the slave-power.

The abolition of slavery is, however, but one step of that continuous and progressive change in the industrial condition of mankind which is due to Christianity. The end is not yet. That change is seen in four successive stages : first, slavery, in which the capitalist owns the laborer ; second, feudalism, in which the capitalist owns the land and has a lien upon the laborer, who is attached to the land ; third, individualism, in which the laborer is free to come and go where and as he will, and competition is relied upon to equalize and adjust property rights and the distribution of wealth ; fourth, the wages-system, under which a few men become the owners of all implements of industry, including the land, the great highways of commerce, and, under our patent laws, the great forces of nature, and the many use these implements of industry in productive toil for such wages as can be agreed upon by the two parties. This is not worse than slavery, as it is sometimes said to be, but infinitely better, — if for no other reason, because the workingman is free. Nor will Ruskin and Carlyle be able to carry us back to the feudal system, with its pseudo-charity and its real oppression. Yet neither is it the finished kingdom of God. A system of industry under which one man may acquire in a lifetime as much money as Adam could have laid by out of his earnings, if he had lived till our time and saved one hundred dollars each working day, is not a perfected system of human brotherhood. A system under which men and women have to work twelve or fourteen hours a day in order to earn bread enough to sustain life; under which little children are set to work when they should be at school; under which Eve, worn out by the burden of child-bearing, has also to bear Adam's burden of ill-remunerated toil; under which God's universal gifts to his children, — fresh air, sunlight, pure water, and the soil, — are denied to hundreds of thousands, who are doomed to a life of drudgery in unsanitary conditions, and without hope of self-improvement, this is not the ideal brotherhood which the Master came to establish upon the earth. Nor will that brotherhood be established until the democracy of political power, founded on a democracy of religion and education, shall be accompanied by an industrial democracy; until the tool workers have become also the tool owners, and class antagonisms are settled by the simple expedient of making the same class both capitalist and laborer; until labor of brain and hand counts for more than money in the world's market, and the present aphorism of political economy is revolutionized, and capital, not labor, money not men, is the commodity to be hired in the cheapest market.

If to any of my readers these seem revolutionary sentences, I can only remind them of the accusation brought against Paul and his associates, " They have turned the world upside down ; " and add my conviction that the accusation was quite true. Christianity is turning the world upside down, and will not cease so to do until the world is right-side up. That all service is honorable and all idleness is a disgrace ; that to get money by whatever strategy without furnishing an equivalent is a dishonorable spoliation ; that wealth is a trust, and that men are to be measured, not by what they possess, but by what use they make of it ; that things are for men, not men for things, and that any civilization is wasteful which grinds up men and women to make cheap goods ; that industry is not righteously organized until it is so organized that every honest and willing worker can find work, and find work so remunerative as to give him and his children an opportunity for self-development as well as for mere life — these are some of the axioms of the Christianity of Jesus Christ.

The evolution of Christianity will not be complete until on these principles the social and industrial structure of modern society is built, and there is much for the reformer to do before this consummation is finally and fully accomplished.

CHAPTER VII.

THE EVOLUTION OF THE SOUL.

How does man come to a divine manhood? Is the process of redemption consistent with the doctrine of evolution? Can the doctrine of redemption be stated in the terms of an evolutionary philosophy? Christlieb has said that the whole Christian creed can be stated in two words, sin and salvation. Are these two articles of our common Christian faith consistent with the doctrine that all life, spiritual as well as physical, proceeds by a "continuous progressive change, according to certain laws, and by means of resident forces"? If not, Christian faith and evolutionary philosophy are inconsistent, and we must conclude either that evolutionary philosophy is false; that Christian faith is false; or that spiritual life is not subject to the law of all other forms of life. For any belief which eliminates these two articles, sin and salvation, from the Christian creed destroys it altogether. It may leave us theists, but not Christians.

The evolutionary philosophy is certainly not consistent with the popular statement of either sin or salvation. That statement is briefly this: God made man perfect. By an act of voluntary disobedience man fell. As a result of that fall, all his descendants became either depraved, *i. e.*, inherently inclined to sin (the New School theory), or sinful, *i. e.*, inherently guilty before God and deserving of his condemnation, independent of any voluntary conscious act committed by the individual (the Old School theory). From this lost and ruined condition, produced by Adam's Fall, man is to be restored to that perfect condition in which he was originally created. By this process of grace, either all men will be restored to Adamic perfection (Universalism) ; or a certain number of men specially selected for such restoration by God, the rest of whom he has been pleased to pass by (Calvinism) ; or a certain number self-selected, namely, all who choose to repent of their sin and accept Christ in this life (Arminianism) ; or in addition, those who, not having understood the terms of salvation in this life, receive and accept them in a life to come (the Doctrine of Future Probation) ; or finally, all those who, without ever having heard of divine grace, possess such character and disposition that they would have accepted the divine grace if they had known about it (Modern New England Theology). This restoration is, at least in its inception, an instantaneous act. It is in no sense a gradual change. The subject of it passes at once from darkness into the light, as one emerges at a given instant, in a swiftly moving train, from a tunnel into the sunshine, or wakes from a long sleep to find the room flooded with daylight. Formerly the soul was expected to know the month, day, hour, of the transition. If he did not, his conversion was looked upon with suspicion. Theologians still generally regard the change as instantaneous, though it is practically conceded that in a majority of cases the time of the change cannot be definitely known. The soul creeps back into Eden and knows not when it has passed the cherubim with the flaming sword. The wilderness has become so blossoming and joyful that the transition is not marked. But the commonly accepted theory remains the same: an original state of perfection; a fall by a representative of the race; a consequent universal condition of sinfulness; and a restoration to that state from which the race fell. [1]

[1] This view is not always, nor indeed generally, consistently held. A friend of mine a few years ago heard a sermon in a back country district, in which the preacher contended that Adam was made acquainted by direct revelation with all that modern discovery and invention has given to us, that his knowledge was passed down by tradition to his descendants, that it was gradually lost as a result of the Fall, that this

Now the doctrine of the Fall and of redemption, *as thus stated*, is inconsistent with the doctrine of evolution. It is impossible to reconcile the two. Evolution declares that all life begins at a lower stage and issues through a gradual development into a higher; the theology just described affirms that man was made at the highest stage and fell to the lower: evolution declares that life is a continuous and progressive change; this theology, that spiritual life always begins in an instantaneous transformation: evolution, that each stage in the process of life is a step into a new life never before possessed; this theology, that the end of all spiritual progress is a return to a life once possessed, now lost. Evolution is quite consistent with theism, — with the doctrine that God made the world and rules over it, working out his purposes of love; with the doctrine that the world

traditional knowledge was the secret of the so-called "lost arts," and that the human race, through redemption, is gradually recovering the intelligence as well as the moral and spiritual perfection originally enjoyed by Adam and Eve. Few theologians, however, would now take so consistent a view as this; the original doctrine of fall and salvation is generally combined in modern preaching with a doctrine of quasi evolution both intellectual and moral; the concession is made to the spirit of the age, that in many respects the modern Nineteenth Century Anglo-Saxon is superior to our First Parents. I am not aware of any attempt to reconcile this modern view with the doctrine of the Fall in its original form.

is gradually growing better under the ministry of his gracious and loving presence. But to many it seems, as it once seemed to me, inconsistent with the two cardinal doctrines of the Christian faith, — sin and salvation; to deny the two most fundamental tenets of Christian revelation and of Christian experience; to reduce sin to a mere imperfection and immaturity; and redemption to a mere process of growth and ripening.

If I were still of the same opinion, I should not be a Christian evolutionist. For philosophy must take account of all the phenomena of life; and a substantially universal consciousness testifies to the reality of sin and remorse. No philosophy can be true which ignores this testimony. I accept the evolutionary philosophy as an interpretation of the spiritual life, because I have come to believe that, rightly apprehended, it gives a more rational and self-consistent interpretation to the great facts of sin and redemption than did the unevolutionary philosophy which accounted for sin by the Fall of our first parents, and made redemption consist of a restoration to the condition which they had lost. The reader will pardon me if, in stating the grounds of my present convictions on this subject, I state in an autobiographical form the process by which I was led to them.

When the evolutionary philosophy first began to be discussed in theological circles, the progressive theologians put all their strength into a discussion of the relation of evolution to theism. They showed, and as it seemed to me showed conclusively, not only that the two were not inconsistent, but that evolution gave a grander view, both of creation and providence, than did the old philosophy, which made the one an instantaneous act and the other a constant interference. But the real question, the relation of evolution to redemption, they did not discuss at all.[1] Jesus Christ came into the world to save sinners. If there were no sinners, only immature men, how could there be either a salvation or a Saviour? And clearly, sin and immaturity are not the same. The immaturity of a child is charming. Who would desire to see him a little old man? But the willful wickedness of a child is not charming; it is odious. Evolution, in denying, as it logically must, the doctrine of the fall of the race in Adam, seemed to me to deny the common sinfulness of the race, which I had been accustomed to trace back to Adam's Fall. Being accustomed all my life to gather my theology from the Bible, I went to the Bible to

---

[1] I desire to express my indebtedness for the first light I received on this subject to an address delivered by Dr. R. W. Raymond before the Congregational Club of New York city.

make a fresh investigation of this subject. In this investigation it was early made clear to me that the Bible lays no such stress upon the Fall as the ecclesiastical systems have done. There is an account of the Fall in the third chapter of Genesis; but elsewhere in the Old Testament, no direct reference to it. The law does not mention it; the Old Testament historians do not refer to it; the poets and the prophets do not so much as allude to it.[1] In the New Testament the reticence is equally marked and significant. Christ never mentions Adam's Fall. Neither does John, nor Jude, nor Peter. Neither Peter nor Paul refers to it in their reported sermons. Paul once gives an account of it in one of his Epistles; but that in a parenthesis. The whole parenthesis might be taken out, and the argument would be unaffected, save by the loss of an incidental illustration. In two or three other passages he refers to it incidentally, as in the phrase, " As in Adam all die, even so in Christ shall all be made alive." But he never treats it as a fundamental and essential fact. In his opening chapter of the Epistle to the

---

[1] The only Old Testament references given to the Fall by the Westminster Confession of Faith, apart from Gen. iii., are Ecclesiastes vii. 29; Psalm li. 5; Job xiv. 4; xv. 14; Jeremiah xvii. 9. Some of these references indicate certainly hereditary depravity, but no one of them, unless Ecclesiastes vii. 29, even remotely suggests a Fall.

Romans, where he brings his terrible indictment against Jew and Gentile, that he may show that all the world is guilty before God, though he gathers both from observation of life and the Old Testament material for this indictment, he makes no reference to any doctrine of a Fall. His only references to it are in arguments addressed to a people who already believed in it, and are made for the purpose of showing them that grace must be as universal as the race, because sin is as universal. This investigation made it first of all clear to me that, whether the doctrine of Adam's Fall were true or not, it occupied in the theology of the Bible no such place of prominence as it has occupied since in the scholastic systems of theology.

Pursuing this inquiry further, I began to ask myself who wrote the account of the Fall in Genesis, and how in literature should this account be classified. The book in which this account is found is quite anonymous; there is no word in it to indicate who is its author. An ancient tradition attributes it to Moses; modern scholarship to an unknown author many centuries subsequent to Moses. If we accept the ancient tradition and attribute the book to the most ancient date assigned to it by any scholar, and then accept the chronology given in the margins of our English Bibles, the history was written twenty-five centuries after the fall of Adam occurred. How did the writer obtain his knowledge of the event? He was not present, nor is there any reason to suppose that Adam or Eve wrote the narrative. It is not, then, the testimony of an eyewitness. Did God reveal the facts to the historian? The historian makes no claim to have received any such revelation. Presumptively he gathered his materials, as other historians gather theirs, from such sources as were accessible to him, — legends, myths, traditions. This presumption is strengthened by the fact that such materials are found in ancient legends of other nations and in the Chaldean tablets, whose age is at least as great as that of the Book of Genesis. It is further strengthened by a careful scrutiny of the Book of Genesis, which has enabled the scholars to separate it, hypothetically, into the narratives of which it was composed. It receives additional confirmation from the nature of the story of Eden, which, if found anywhere save in Hebrew literature, would at once be characterized by the reader as poetic and imaginative, not as scientific and historical. Finally, separating the Book of Genesis into its component parts, I found that in one of the narratives of which it is composed, — the one containing the incomparable account of the creation embodied in the first chapter of Genesis,

— there was nowhere, directly or indirectly, any reference to an Eden or a Fall. It thus became very clear to me that the doctrine, " In Adam's Fall, we sinned all," which was the first item of theology taught me in my childhood, is not the fundamental doctrine which I had once held it to be ; that, on the contrary, it furnishes a very unsubstantial foundation for the elaborate theological superstructure which has been reared upon it. It took me some years of study and reflection to reach this conclusion, and it will not be strange, if the reader, accustomed to think that the doctrine of the Fall is woven into the very structure of the Bible, because he has found it woven into the very structure of the creeds, is slow to accept at my hands this contrary conclusion ; but I must here assume it as established, and go on to a further investigation of the question what light philosophy and science throw upon the origin and nature of man, and upon the phenomena of sin and remorse, of pardon and peace.

What, then, is man ? and what his origin and the law of his development ?

Comparative physiology and anatomy make it clear that he is an animal ; sub-kingdom, vertebrate ; class, mammal ; order, apes. Whatever the historic origin of the race, embryology makes it clear that the origin of each individual of the race is animal, and that he passes in the earlier stage of his existence through processes of development analogous to, if not precisely the same as, those through which other animals of the same general class and order pass. Comparative philology and scientific anthropology, so far as we can trace animal life back to prehistoric periods, lead towards the conclusion that all races of men not only have a common origin, but one in common with other kindred animals. Finally this conclusion is confirmed by the general results of investigation in other departments of life, — material, animal, social, political, historical, — which have led substantially all scientific students to the conclusion that all life proceeds by a " continuous progressive change, according to certain laws, and by means of resident forces."

The objections to the theory that man himself has been developed in accordance with this law from a lower animal order are four, — the sentimental, the scientific, the Biblical, and the religious.

The sentimental is expressed by the now familiar joke: So, you think your grandfather was an ape? But to have ascended from an ape is not more ignominious than to have ascended from a clay man. Whether God has put a divine spirit into the animal man is a question of fundamental religious significance, and we will consider it presently: but how he prepared this animal habitation for the indwelling of the divine spirit, whether by an instantaneous creative act or by a gradual evolutionary process, is a question with no religious significance whatever. It is to be determined wholly by scientific considerations.

The scientific objection is that there are gaps both in historical and in physiological continuity; that, on the one hand, the famous " missing link " between primitive man and the ape has never been found by geological research; and, on the other, that to-day the difference between the brain capacity of man and that of the ape constitutes a gap which the evolutionary hypothesis is unable to bridge, — a difference freely and frankly admitted by the greatest exponents of evolution.[1] It is not necessary

[1] Thus Darwin, in *The Descent of Man:* " We have seen in the last chapter that man bears in his bodily structure clear traces of his descent from some lower form; but it may be urged that, as man differs so greatly in his mental power from all other animals, there must be some error in this conclusion. No doubt the difference in this respect is enormous, even if we compare the mind of one of the lowest savages, who has no words to express any number higher than four, and who uses no abstract terms for the commonest objects or affections, with that of the most highly organized ape. The difference would, no doubt, still remain immense, even if one of the higher apes had been improved or civilized as much as a dog has been in comparison with its parent-form, the wolf or

for me here to reproduce the scientific answer
to this objection, for this is not a scientific trea-
tise. It must suffice to say that he who is not
a scientific expert must be content to await
the final judgment of those who are experts on
this subject, and meanwhile accept tentatively
their conclusion; and that conclusion, arrived
at with substantial unanimity by all who have
investigated this subject, is that the scientific
objections to the doctrine of the evolution of
man from a lower animal order are insignificant
in comparison with the evidence in support of
that hypothesis and the objections to any other.
Thus Le Conte, himself a Christian believer, declares that " evolution, therefore, is no longer
a school of thought. The words *evolutionism*
and *evolutionist* ought not any longer to be

jackal. The Fuegians rank among the lowest barbarians;
but I was continually struck with surprise how closely the
three natives on board H. M. S. Beagle, who had lived
some years in England, and could talk a little English, resem-
bled us in disposition, and in most of our mental faculties."
(Vol. i. 133.) Similarly Huxley, in *Evidences as to Man's Place
in Nature :* "It must not be overlooked, however, that there
is a very striking difference in absolute mass and weight between the lowest human brain and that of the highest ape —
a difference which is all the more remarkable when we recol-
lect that a full grown Gorilla is probably pretty nearly twice
as heavy as a Bosjes man, or as many an European woman.
It may be doubted whether a healthy human adult brain ever
weighed less than thirty one or two ounces, or that the heavi-
est Gorilla brain has exceeded twenty ounces " (p. 231).

used, any more than gravitationism and gravitationist; for the law of evolution is as certain as the law of gravitation. Nay, it is far more certain." In view of such a statement from such a source, it is decorous for the non-expert in science to pass by without discussion the scientific objection to the doctrine.

The Biblical objection I have already considered; the religious or spiritual objection deserves some further consideration. This objection is, in brief, that evolution degrades and dishonors man; denies the divinity in him; despoils him alike of his divine parentage, his present hopes and expectations, and his immortal future; reduces him from a child of God to a child of the beast. If this were true, it would be conclusive. For consciousness is the final factor in the determination of every problem; and no scientific hypothesis could be true which set itself against the testimony of consciousness bearing witness to every man that there is in him a divine personality and an illimitable destiny.

Man is an animal; but he is more than an animal. To say of a man, "He is a perfect brute," is not to pay him the highest possible compliment. Nor is the difference between him and the highest animals one of physical peculiarities merely. A two-handed ape would not

be a man, nor a four-footed man an ape. Each
would be simply a freak of nature. Nor is it
that one possesses only instinct, and the other
reason. Philosophy has long since abandoned
the endeavor to maintain that sharp distinction
between reason and instinct which was assumed
by the older philosophies. Observation has
noted many illustrations of reasoning power, of
a limited degree, in the higher animals.[1]

But one looks in vain in the animal race for
those moral and spiritual elements which are
characteristic of men. The conscience of the
dog is caught from his master, and he can with
equal facility be taught that it is a virtue or a
vice to steal. Reverence for invisible qualities
or for an invisible power is rarely, if ever, want-
ing in even the lowest types of manhood, and

---

[1] The books are full of well-authenticated instances of
reasoning in dogs, horses, and elephants. One, if I remember
aright, told by Philip Gilbert Hamerton, may serve as a type.
A spaniel, who had been taught that he must not go upon the
garden beds, was observed attempting to drive a hen and
chickens from the garden. They ran among the beds, while
he ran round the beds, from path to path, in a vainly wild attempt to expel them. Suddenly he was seen to drop down in
the path with his nose between his paws, as if in meditation;
then to spring suddenly again to his feet, make a dart, catch
one of the chickens in his mouth and start for the garden gate.
The mother ran clucking after him, the brood followed her.
Once outside the gate he dropped the chicken unharmed, and
trotted up to the house, wagging his tail. If this was not reason, what was it?

never discoverable in the highest type of the animals. Worship of some sort is substantially universal with mankind, and unknown except among mankind. The ants have their slaves, the bees their warehouses, the beavers their colonies; but nowhere sign of temple, priesthood, or worship. In men alone is there the possibility of illimitable development. The end of education in the best trained animal is soon reached. Every new acquirement of man adds to his moral and intellectual power and increases his moral intelligence. He carries in himself the evidence that he is of kin to the Infinite, because he never reaches enduring satisfaction in what he has secured, but ever finds therein a new incentive to seek something yet to come. Thus the animal is, while man never is, but always is becoming. Whence did he receive this divine, this immortal, this undying, this illimitable life? Is the author of the first chapter of Genesis correct? Did God at some moment in man's upward career, by an instantaneous act, breathe the breath of a divine life into man? Or are we to accept the theory of the radical evolutionists, as interpreted by Le Conte and Darwin, and believe that this higher nature of man was developed out of the lower animal instincts, as the body of men out of an earlier and inferior form? This latter hypothesis must be regarded as yet among the un-proved hypotheses of science ; with more at present, it seems to me, against than for it. But the question is one of science, not of reli-gion, and we may well leave it for science to determine. Religion has to do with the present and the future, not with the past, — save as it disentangles us from the past for the future. It knows but three words, Duty, Destiny, God. Religion may well leave science to determine the question where man came from, and devote itself to the question what man is and what he can become. The candid reader, desirous only of the truth, will gladly recognize that the most skeptical of evolutionists affirms the existence in man of moral and spiritual qualities which differentiate him from the animal, and agrees with the orthodox believer that man possesses a divine nature and a divine destiny.

Says Mr. Huxley : " I have endeavored to show that no absolute structural line of demarca-tion, wider than that between the animals which immediately succeed us in the scale, can be drawn between the animal world and ourselves ; and I may add the expression of my belief that the attempt to draw a physical distinction is equally futile, and that even the highest facul-ties of feeling and of intellect begin to germinate in lower forms of life. At the same time, no one is more strongly convinced than I am of the vastness of the gulf between civilized man and the brutes; or is more certain that, whether from them or not, he is assuredly not of them. No one is less disposed to think lightly of the present dignity, or despairingly of the future hopes, of the only consciously intelligent denizen of this world. We are indeed told by those who assume authority in these matters that the two sets of opinions are incompatible, and that the belief in the unity of origin of man and brutes involves the brutalization and degradation of the former. But is this really so? Could not a sensible child confute, by obvious arguments, the shallow rhetoricians who would force this conclusion upon us? Is it indeed true that the poet, or the philosopher, or the artist, whose genius is the glory of his age, is degraded from his high estate by the undoubted historical probability, not to say certainty, that he is the direct descendant of some naked and bestial savage, whose intelligence was just sufficient to make him a little more cunning than the fox, and by so much more dangerous than the tiger? Or is he bound to howl and grovel on all fours because of the wholly unquestionable fact that he was once an egg, which no ordinary power of discrimination could distinguish from that of a dog? Or is the philanthropist

or the saint to give up his endeavors to lead a
noble life because the simplest study of man's
nature reveals, at its foundations, all the selfish
passions and fierce appetites of the merest qua-
druped? Is mother-love vile, because a hen
shows it; or fidelity base, because dogs possess
it? . . . Our reverence for the nobility of manhood will not be lessened by the knowledge that
man is in substance and in structure one with
the brutes; for he alone possesses the marvel-
ous endowment of intelligible and rational
speech, whereby, in the secular period of his existence, he has slowly accumulated and organized
the experience which is almost wholly lost with
the cessation of every individual life in other
animals; so that now he stands raised upon it,
as on a mountain-top, far above the level of
his humble fellows, and transfigured from his
grosser nature by reflecting here and there a
ray from the infinite source of truth." [1]

I conclude, then, that the doctrine that man is
developed from a lower animal order is not inconsistent with the teaching of the Bible, if the
Bible be interpreted as itself the history of the
development of religious thought and life, the
life of God in the soul of man, as I have endeavored to interpret it in the second chapter of
this volume; nor is it inconsistent with the spir-

[1] Huxley, *Evidence as to Man's Place in Nature*, page 234.

itual consciousness of man, — his consciousness
of a divine life which makes him more than an
animal and links him to God.

Nor does it militate against the doctrine of
redemption. On the contrary, it gives a nobler
and grander conception of redemption than was
ever afforded by the doctrine of Adam's fall.
For the evolutionist sees in redemption, not a
mere restoration of man to a former state of innocence, but a process of divine development
which, beginning with man just emerging from
the animal condition, carries him forward, from
innocence, through temptation, fall, and sin, into
virtue and holiness. To make this clear, I ask
the reader, laying aside doubtful questionings
as to the prehistoric history and development of
the race, to trace with me in the rest of this
chapter the actual progress of a soul, as we see
it in life, from the cradle to a truly heroic and
saintly manhood.

The babe is innocent. No theology can make
the mother really believe that the soul which
looks trustingly up to her through those eloquent
eyes is guilty, " under the wrath and condemnation of God." But the innocence of the babe
is the innocence of ignorance. It is guiltless of
wrong-doing because it does not know the difference between right and wrong ; innocent, but
lawless ; not yet brought under law. It is a

little animal. It knows only how to suckle and
to cry. It is without power of self-control by
intelligent consciousness and will, because intelligent consciousness and will are not yet evoked.
It is greedy, has no control of its appetite,
clamors and cries for its mother's breast, does
not sip daintily and delicately, but drinks greed-
ily, like every other animal. It is predatory,
by nature a robber, but as innocent in its rob-
bery as the magpie. It sees another baby on
the floor, enjoying a rattle, crawls across, assails
the possessor of the wealth, seizes it, and has no
consciousness of wrong-doing. As it has to learn
how to use eyes and hands and feet, so it has to
learn how to use reason, consciousness, reverence,
love. Little by little it learns that it is in a
world of law. Fire teaches it that some things
cannot be touched with safety; sour or bitter
tastes, that all things cannot be put into the
mouth with comfort. If the mother be wise, the
child early begins to learn, by mother's prohibitions enforced by mother's penalties, that there
are also moral laws. It begins to eat the fruit
of the tree of knowledge of good and evil. Conscience is awakened; and conscience begins to
legislate and to enforce its legislation. Thus by
law comes a knowledge of sin. As the life en-
larges, the experience of law increases. Brothers
and sisters enforce unwritten law. The child

goes to school. The laws of the school-fellows are more numerous and more exacting than the laws of the school-master. Business life creates new relations, and discovers new laws of business honor. Citizenship reveals still another code, or, to speak more accurately, other applications of the one law of love. Marriage introduces the young man to another life, with obligations of chivalry, husband-love and father-love, protection of the weak and the defenseless. Thus each new development of life brings with it a new revelation of duty. In each stage of life the growing man comes to a new Mt. Sinai. And with the growing consciousness of law, enforced by penalties, — paternal, governmental, social, or self-inflicted, — comes an ever-growing sense of right and wrong; an ever-growing consciousness of the praiseworthiness of right conduct and the blameworthiness of wrong conduct. The little animal is growing up into manhood; and the process of this growth is a process in which, by successive stages, it is brought into the consciousness of a moral law, and so into the consciousness of a higher than a mere animal nature.

This process of growth by law, enforced by penalties which are inflicted by authority without or consciousness within, is essential to moral character. And essential to this process of

growth is temptation, that is, the conflict between the higher and the lower nature. Only
through temptation comes virtue, that is, the
subjection of the lower to the higher nature;
and incidental to temptation is sin, that is, the
subjection of the higher nature to the lower.
Without this growth of moral consciousness
— this emergence from the innocence of the
mere animal — neither sin nor virtue is possible.
Gluttony is not sin in a hog; the greater glut-
ton, the better the breed. Combativeness is not
sin in a bull-dog; the bitterer fighter, the better the dog. To heap up wealth for another
to enjoy after they are dead is not sin in the
bees; the more they gather and the less they
give, the more valuable the hive. To spend life
in the mere pleasure of song and sunshine is
not sin in the bird; the more careless the song-
ster, the sweeter is his companionship. But to
man there is a higher life possible than to feed
with the hog, fight with the dog, gather with the
bee, or sing with the birds; it is as he comes to
a knowledge of this higher nature that he comes
to a knowledge of good and evil; it is as the
higher nature becomes victor over the lower that
he comes to a life of true virtue.

It is conceivable that man might go on this
pilgrimage upward and onward from the animal
to the intellectual and moral life without a lapse,

that is, without that degeneration which, as we have seen,[1] the scientists recognize as incidental to evolution. But in fact man never thus progresses. He deliberately, and again and again, turns his back upon the higher life, and goes down into the lower life from which he has emerged. The self-indulgent appetite, the unregulated passion, the blind and uninspired acquisitiveness, the surrender to selfish pleasure-seeking, is a recurrence to the animal nature from which the voice of reason, of conscience, of reverence, — that is, of God, — has summoned him. To call this recurrence to the animal nature, this degeneration from the spiritual to the sensual, a " step in advance " is to confound the obstacles to progress with the progress which they hinder and delay. In every such lapse there is a true fall ; and we so recognize it in the common language of our daily life. If a theretofore honest and honorable man, yielding to some great temptation, has embezzled or defaulted, we speak of him as having fallen ; and a " fallen woman " is the common designation of one whose lapse has been sudden from a position of the highest purity to one of sensual degradation. Whether Adam fell six thousand years ago, by eating the fruit of a forbidden tree, is a debatable question, on which

[1] See chap. i. p. 10.

really little depends. Every man falls when, by yielding to the enticements of his lower, animal nature, he descends from his vantage-ground of moral consciousness to the earthiness out of which he had begun to emerge.

Thus, in the view of the Christian evolutionist, sin is not mere unripeness and immaturity which growth and sunshine will cure. It is a deliberate disobedience of the divine law, into the knowledge of which the soul has come in its emergence from the animal condition.

And fall is not an historic act of disobedience by the parents of our race in some prehistoric age, through which a sinful nature has descended or been imparted to all their descendants. It is the conscious and deliberate descent of the individual soul from the vantage ground of a higher life to the life of the animal from which he had been uplifted.

And redemption is not the restoration of the race to that state of innocence from which it has departed; it is the entire process of intellectual and spiritual development in which man passes, by means of law and temptation, through the possibility of sin and fall, from the condition of innocence, that is, of ignorance of law and therefore exemption from guilt, into the condition of virtue, that is, into a conscious recognition of law, and the subjugation of the animal self to the higher nature which law and temptation have evoked.[1] Something more remains to be said in the next chapter of this process of redemption from the point of view of the Christian evolutionist.

[1] It may be observed, incidentally, that this statement affords an interpretation of such declarations concerning Christ as that he " was in all points tempted like as we are, yet without sin," that he, as the captain of our salvation, was made " perfect through suffering," and that he " increased in wisdom and stature and in favor with God and man." These and kindred declarations indicate that he passed from the innocence of infancy to the virtue of manhood, through the pathway of law and temptation, exactly as all other men; with this one radical difference, that as far as he came to a knowledge of righteousness he fulfilled righteousness; he never disobeyed, and so never lapsed or fell.

CHAPTER VIII.

THE SECRET OF SPIRITUAL EVOLUTION.

VIRTUE, the conscious recognition of a moral law and the conscious and deliberate conformity to it, is not the consummation of character. There is something still higher. The law of the spiritual life is not truly the law of the soul until wrought into the nature itself. Then virtue becomes the second nature. The man no longer by deliberate acts of the will conforms to a standard external to himself; he is not subject to law, but is himself an embodied law; becomes a law unto himself; does whatever he pleases because he pleases to do whatever is right. Thus, in that spiritual evolution which constitutes redemption, man passes through three stages: in the first he is lawless but innocent, and in his ignorance of the law he is controlled by his animal impulses;[1] in the second stage he recognizes the higher law of his nascent divine nature, and endeavors to conform his life and

[1] He is by nature the child of wrath (Ephes. ii. 3), not of God's wrath, but of his own unregulated appetites and passions.

character to it; in the third stage this law has become the law of his being, and he lives in peace and liberty, because his impulses have themselves become spiritual impulses. The first stage is innocence; the second is virtue; the third is holiness.

What is the secret power by which this revolution, or, if the reader prefers, this evolution, in character is wrought? The process is growth; but what is the power?

Life gives to this question a very plain answer. The power which effects transformations in character is the power of another personality. This is the power recognized in all systems of education: the power of the teacher, inciting, inspiring, moulding the pupil. This is the power of the true orator, who moves his audience less by what he says, or the method of his saying it, than by what he is. His speech is only the expression of himself; and it is not the expression, nor the thought expressed, but the *person*, expressed in and through the thought and the speech, which moves and shapes the audience to the orator's will. This is the power of the musician; the difference between the true musician and the mere performer being that the latter has only technique, while the former has also what we call soul; music is but the method which that soul takes to utter itself.

This makes great leaders great. The presence of the "Little Corporal" is worth a battalion of soldiers, because by his mere presence he infuses his own invincible courage into all his army, and re-creates it by his military spirit. This is the secret of the mother's influence; this gives value to her training. Instruction in methods cannot make, and ignorance of methods cannot mar. If the mother has a true spirit of motherly devotion, if she has piety and truth and courage and self-sacrifice, these will find their expression, and the child will be formed less by what his mother deliberately designs than by what in her inmost being she is.

The secret of the world's moral evolution is such a personality, brooding all mankind; uttering itself through all history in "broken lights" and transitory gleams; uttering itself through Hebrew history by "divers portions and in divers manners;" and finally and perfectly incarnate in the Christ.

Who, then, was the Christ? And what is his relation to the religious life, — the life of God in the soul of men?

Theological controversies about the Christ are not in Christ's spirit, nor do they tend to promote reverence for his person or his life, nor help to bring any soul into a greater love or a truer following of him. Into these controversies

I mean never to enter. Nor have I any psychology of his unique personality to offer to myself or others, nor any definition of his relations to the Infinite and the Eternal. All our knowledge of truth is relative: I say our *knowledge* of truth, not truth itself. What matter is, no man can tell. We can understand only its relations to ourselves. What spirit is, no man can tell. We can understand it only as it appears in and to ourselves. What Jesus Christ is to the infinite and eternal Father, I make no attempt to discuss. I consider only what he is to the individual soul, and what he has been to the human race. He is himself the answer to the two great questions of our spiritual life: What is man? Who is God?

These are the profoundest questions that ever addressed themselves to the human soul. What am I, and what is my destiny? — not what am I now, still less where did I come from, but what are the possibilities within me, and what the life that beckons me on to an illimitable life? What will be evolved out of me when the work of growth is over? — that is the real question. If the Christian church had spent half the time in studying the problem how it could get on, which it has spent in debating the question whether it came from Adam or not, it would have made much further progress than it has.

Evolution is the development of any object towards the fulfillment of the end of its being; and by a force resident in the object itself. What I may become depends in the last analysis upon what is the power within me — the power which by my free acceptance I take, and so cause to be within me. If I were not a free moral agent, it would not be important for me to ask this question; but I am a free moral agent. The seed does not ask, Shall I become a rose or a pear? because the seed will become whatever the soil and the sunshine and its original nature make it. But just because I am a free moral agent I must work with God, and what I become, whether rose or thistle, depends — I say it reverently — as truly on myself as on him. I am not a flute, out of which he can draw what music he likes; I am not plastic clay on the revolving table, which he fashions into what he likes; I am not a movable type which he puts where he likes. There is in me a power, and that power must coöperate with him, or there will be no music in my life, no divine figure wrought, no divine truth printed. Now, if I am to coöperate with God, if he and I are in partnership, if I must toil with him as the teacher toils with his pupil or the mother with the child, I must know who and what I am to be. I must be able to ask him, What sort of a utensil are you purposing to make? We must work together, and therefore we must understand each another.

To this great question of questions, What is man? — not in his present condition, but in his future possibility — Jesus Christ furnishes the answer. He does not furnish the answer in detail. Not even Christ is to be blindly and servilely imitated. You cannot ask him what are the peculiar duties of a wife to a husband, or of a husband to a wife, for he never was married; how you are to treat children, for he never had children; how you are to vote in the coming election — he never cast a vote; how you shall treat your customers and clerks — he was no merchant. It almost seems as if the details of life were left out of his experiences in order that we might not follow in detail any life, not even his. We follow Christ as every ship that crosses the ocean from Spain to America follows Columbus, marking none the less a special pathway for itself, — each going in its own course, yet each following to a common goal. He came to give life, and he gave it abundantly, and for fullness of life there must be individuality. He makes us live, not by directing us to hew ourselves to a precise and particular pattern, but by showing every man how he may be his own best self. None the less, but rather far

more, for this reason, he answered the question,
What is man? for he is the type of manhood.

He was a Jew, and yet he was the reverse of
a Jew — unworldly, catholic, free. He was born
in the Orient, but he was not characteristically
Oriental, — no dreamer or visionary, he. His
religion was one of practical, every-day life.
He transcends even the limitations of sex. Man
he was, yet with all the patience, gentleness,
and tenderness we attribute to woman; but who
will think of calling him that poorest and weak-
est of creatures, a womanly man? He transcends all ages, and is the ideal of to-day as he
was the ideal in the first century. He fought
no battles, yet Havelock reads the story of his
life and is quickened in courage. He nursed no
sick, yet the nurses in a thousand hospitals find
the inspiration of their patient toil in the story
of his patient life. He was no merchant, and
yet he was the exemplar of our Amos Lawrence
and our Cooper. He was no statesman, yet
Gladstone is his follower. All men find alike
in this one unique and incomparable figure the
one worthy of their following, the type of their
manhood. He was not a man, but *the* man,
filling full the ideal of a complete manhood.
Do we not idealize him? No, we have not ideal-
ized Jesus Christ. Jesus Christ is engaged in
idealizing us, and the work is not completed.

As he answers the one great question of our lives, What is man? so, he answers the other great question of our lives, Who is God? The great factor in human reformation is divine personality. But, if we are to be moulded by a person, we must know who that person is. Do we want to know about God, or do we want personally to be acquainted *with* God? These are two different questions. In the one, curiosity asks for the measurement of him; in the other, reverence and love ask for personal fellowship with him. Only curiosity can be satisfied by an ambassador, a prophet, a teacher. Out of that Roman conception of theology which made God an eternal Cæsar and men his subjects grew by a natural process the conception of Jesus Christ as an ambassador from God to man. But if God is not a king whose laws we are to understand, but a Father whose heart I need to know, then no revelation of teacher, be he human, angelic, or superangelic, will suffice. It is the Person himself I need to know. I cannot love by proxy. No account, philosophical and skillful though it may be, of the attributes of God suffices as a foundation for love toward God. Tell me he is perfect in wisdom, power, love, mercy; these are but attributes: it is himself I want to know. The cry of the human being from the earliest age — the cry of Job,

" Oh that I knew where I might find him ! " —
is still the cry of humanity. All history is the
search after God. All science, whether the scientist knows it or not, is the thinking of the
thoughts of God after him, the trying to find
him. All art is the search after the ideal art as
it exists in some true, divine artist. All love —
of lover, wife, husband, child, patriot — is but
the fragmentary and imperfect expression of the
Infinite and Eternal All-loving. All men have
at the hearts of them more or less of this hunger and desire to know the Infinite and the
Eternal. To this hunger Christ is the answer,
to this " cry of the human " he is the response
of the divine.

Let us consider, for one moment, that God is
training children to be free like himself, and by
their own free choice to become partakers of his
nature ; that he can do this only by impressing
his own personality upon them ; and that he can
impress that personality upon them only by
manifesting himself to them. Are there not
just three ways in which he can do this, and
only three ? — to the intellect, to the sensibili-
ties, and to the will ? Must he not either by
his works show himself to the thought of man,
or by his personal presentation in life show himself to the affections of man, or by his personal
contact with man, bringing him into obedience

to himself, show himself to the will of man? How can Arnold of Rugby be known? Is there any way but these three? We know his school, and so we know something of the work he has done. We read the story of his life, and we see the personality of the man. We sit at his table and talk with him; our life becomes intertwined with his; we enter into sorrow or joy and work together with him. Deism gives us intellectual knowledge of God — we know him through his works. Theism gives us knowledge of him through his will entering our life and our attempt to follow out his will as it is interpreted in our own conscience. The faith of the ages in the Christian church gives us these; but it gives us also the other element, a Person manifesting God on the earth — God interpreted in terms of human biography, in order that we may see and know and love him. Corresponding with these three ways of knowing God are the three great historical religions, each of which serves as a representative of the three religions which are now clamoring in America for our suffrages — ethical culture, mysticism, and historical Christianity. Ethical culture, which claims to know that there is a right and wrong, but can discover no eternal basis for it in a Personal and Eternal Lawgiver, has produced China. Mysticism, which perceives God only as he is immanent in every human soul, but discovers no objective and historical manifestation of him, has produced India. And historical Christianity, with its triune manifestation of God, in nature, in human consciousness, and in the one sacred and unique Life, has produced Europe. By their fruits ye shall know them.

It has been sometimes said in orthodox literature that Jesus Christ was God ; but that statement in the New Testament is always accompanied by limitations — the Word of God made flesh, God tabernacling among us, The image of God's person, The brightness of God's glory. Jesus Christ is, in other words, represented as God reducing himself to finite proportions and walking in finite relations, that we may comprehend him whom otherwise we could not comprehend. The doctrine of the church is explicit in its recognition of the truth expressed by Paul in his declaration of Christ's " self-beggary " in order that he might enter into humanity and fill it with the riches of his nature.

Thus to these two questions of the human soul Jesus Christ is the answer. What is man ? — He is the ideal of manhood. Who is God ? — What Jesus Christ was, in the limit of a few years' time and in the little province of Palestine, that is the Infinite and Eternal Father in his dealings with the universe.

It is said by one class of critics that the doctrine of the evolution of Christianity necessarily involves the belief that Jesus Christ was himself a product of evolution; and as there have been over eighteen centuries of spiritual evolution since Christ's time, it involves a presumption that there are other products of spiritual evolution superior to him, or at least that there will be such superior products in the future. If the evolutionist denies this, if he claims to believe in the divinity of Jesus Christ, or, using the very inadequate language of theological metaphysics, in his supernatural character, then it is said that he believes in evolution "with an if;" that he is not a consistent evolutionist, but makes an exception. Now if either of these statements were true, the result would be fatal to the philosophy which underlies this book. If the Christian evolutionist regards Jesus Christ as a product of spiritual evolution, he gives up Christianity, not merely as an ideal of life, but as a philosophy. He may still be a devout theist; but he is in no *philosophical* sense a Christian. If on the other hand he declares that Jesus Christ is an exception to the law of evolution, he gives up evolution; for God's laws are not like the laws of Greek grammar, with exceptions. When science seeks to formulate a law of life, it succeeds only in case the law provides for all the phenomena of life. If some of these phenomena are inconsistent with the supposed law, the supposed law does not exist. A single established exception to the law of gravitation would require a re-statement of the law in such terms as would provide for that exception.

Philosophically, Jesus Christ can be regarded by the evolutionist in only one of two ways : as a product or as the producer of evolution. The careful reader will perhaps recall a statement in the introductory chapter of this volume to the effect that evolution does not account for the origin, but only for the processes of life. Even the agnostic evolutionist does not — certainly most agnostic evolutionists do not — consider that life is a product of evolution. Life is a cause ; phenomena are the product; evolution is the method. The theistic evolutionist does not believe that God is a product of evolution. God is the cause ; phenomena are the product ; evolution is the method. So, the Christian evolutionist does not believe that Jesus Christ is the product of evolution. Jesus Christ is the cause ; phenomena are the product; evolution is the method. This is what the Christian evolutionist means by the divinity of Jesus Christ; life, God, Christ, are not synonymous terms, but each of them expresses the finite apprehension of different phases of the Infinite. Life is the Infinite in nature as the scientist sees him, evolving out material phenomena according to the law of growth or evolution; God is the Infinite as the devout soul sees him, evolving out both material and spiritual phenomena according to the laws of growth or evolution; and Christ is the Infinite entering into human life, and taking on the finite, in order that he may achieve the end of all evolution, material and spiritual, in bringing men to know and be at one with God. Does the scientific evolutionist believe in evolution "with an if," because he believes that life — the Infinite and Eternal Energy — is the cause, not the product, of evolution? Does the theist believe in evolution "with an if" because he believes that God is the cause, not the product, of evolution? As little does the Christian evolutionist believe in evolution "with an if," because he believes that Jesus Christ is the cause, not the product, of redemption. Must a man choose whether he will believe in light, or in the sun? As little need he choose whether he will believe in a divine spirit which pervades all life, or in a divine spirit from whom comes light and life into the world. The huntsman with his burning-glass concentrates the diffused rays of the sun upon his fagots and kindles them into a blaze.

In Jesus Christ, the diffused spirit of God, the Infinite and Eternal Energy from whom all things proceed, the Power not ourselves that makes for righteousness, is concentrated in a single human life, and kindles humanity into a blaze of love, imparting to it his own glory.

If my reader will remember the perfectly simple fact that philosophy must in its study always recognize three factors, a cause, a process, and a product, that evolution has to do only with the process, and that the Christian evolutionist regards Jesus Christ as the cause, evolution as the process, and Christianity as the product, however much he may disagree with my interpretation of Christianity, he will at least be saved from a radical misapprehension of it.

To sum up, then, these two chapters in a paragraph: God is in his world of matter and his world of men. He is the Word, — "The Word was with God and the Word was God." That is, from eternity God has been a self-revealing Person. He has been disclosing himself. He has not been like the Egyptian Sphinx; he has from eternity expressed himself in matter by creation, and in human history by the utterances of his prophets and apostles, and in Jesus Christ in *propria persona* has entered human life, in order that he might show us who he is, that so we might have One round whom we might put our arms, before whom we might bow in reverence, to whom we might give our highest, supremest, tenderest love.

CHAPTER IX.

CONCLUSION: THE CONSUMMATION OF SPIRITUAL EVOLUTION.

In this chapter I propose rapidly to survey the ground already traversed, re-state the conclusions reached, and finally re-define, in the language of evolutionary theology, some theological terms in common use.

God is in his world. Nature is not a machine which a mechanic has made, wound up, and set going, and with which he must from time to time interfere, as a watchmaker interferes to regulate a somewhat imperfect time-keeper. Nature is the expression of God's thought, the outward utterance of himself. He dwells in it and works through it. Amid all the mysteries by which we are surrounded, says Herbert Spencer, nothing is more certain than this, that we are ever in the presence of an Infinite and Eternal Energy from which all things proceed. This Infinite and Eternal Energy from which all things proceed is an intelligent Energy. It is an Energy that thinks, and creation is the expression of the thought of this

Infinite and Eternal Energy. Much of the old teleological argument, as it is called, may perhaps be set aside by modern research, and I believe that the notion of secondary causes proceeding from a great First Cause must be set aside. But in the world there is one underlying Cause which is the source and fountain of all power; and the fact that we investigate natural phenomena, and endeavor to see their relations to one another, shows that there are relations in those phenomena which the intellect can comprehend, and which therefore are themselves intellectual. Science is not the mere putting of phenomena in pigeon-holes and setting labels upon them. Science perceives in nature a real thoughtfulness, and follows along the path which preëxisting thought has marked out for it. Even Haeckel, in the very chapter in which he undertakes to show that the notion of a divine Creator behind the creation should be abandoned, repeats on almost every page the language of intellectualism, showing the "purpose" of this, the "object" of that, and the "design" of the other. He cannot speak of the phenomena of the universe, even in the attempt to dethrone God from it, without in his very words showing that there is a Designer, a Thinker, and a Purposer.

This God, whose existence is demonstrated by

the unity in the material universe, is no less demonstrated by the unity of the immaterial universe. There is as truly a science of history and sociology as there is a science of astronomy and of biology; and as nature, so humanity has a unity and a continuity. Mankind are not mere segregated atoms of sand on the beach — there is a moral unity in the human race. All history recognizes this, and evolution brings it out more clearly than it was brought out before. History as a mere record of the separate acts of individuals has passed away, and now the true historian, following the example of those who in the last century first began to write modern history, sees that there is a moral development; that events lead on to other events in the realm of spirit as in the realm of matter; that there is a God in history, as there is a God in nature — a God who is working out some great design among men, as there is a God who is working out great designs through all material and mechanical phenomena.

But God can express himself in terms of moral life — can utter himself in terms of righteousness — only through beings that have the power of righteousness, and therefore through beings that are free to be unrighteous. A man forced to be virtuous is not virtuous at all, for freedom to choose the evil is essential to constitute the good. Thus while in nature God may work out the mechanical evidences of his skill and love of beauty, he can work out the expressions of his truth, purity, and holiness only in a world which has in it a possibility of the reverse.

In such a world as this he is expressing himself, and has expressed himself from the beginning. All men are his children, and all nations are his. But as some men show greater susceptibility to his presence than others, so in some nations he is more manifested than in others; and as he expresses himself more truly in some lives than in others, so in some nations and races he expresses himself more truly than in other nations and races. If you ask why one man seems to be more susceptible to divine influence than another, I answer that I do not know. I take life as I find it, and recognize the fact without offering any explanation. As I do not know why the acorn produces an oak, or why the apple-seed produces an apple-tree, so I do not know why God in one life seems to bring forth results which in another life he does not bring forth. But such is the fact; and our business in a scientific study of human life is to accept the fact.

Among all the nations of antiquity, the one nation which displayed a peculiar genius for

what men call religion — that is, a peculiar
genius for the spiritual and invisible — was the
Hebrew race. As compared with modern races,
the Hebrews often seem dull and obtuse; but
as compared with the nations about them, they
were a nation fitted for the beginning of a manifestation of righteousness. For fifteen centuries
of history, God was dealing with this nation as
with all nations; but in this nation the fruit of
his dealing was manifest as in none other, and
in men of special spiritual genius of this nation
as in no other men. During these fifteen centuries of his dealing with this people, he called
forth their genius, and out of the writings of
their prophets he secured, by what you may call
natural selection or divine providence, according
as you are scientifically or religiously inclined,
a permanent book, the Bible. Thus the Bible
is the expression of God in human thought —
God speaking to men and through men — God
speaking through the selected writings of the
selected prophets of a selected people. When
the ripeness of time had come, this process of
speaking to men issued in the Incarnation —
the speaking of God *in* man. Up to the first
century, the Word had been a word spoken *to*
humanity. In the birth of Jesus Christ, the
Word itself became incarnate : God, who had
expressed himself through men, now expressed

himself in a human life. He entered into humanity, and in Christ Jesus became a sharer of human nature. The Word tabernacled among men became subject to human conditions, shared the weaknesses, the wants, the ignorance of humanity.

For what purpose ? Simply to manifest himself to men ? Such a manifestation, if it led to nothing, would give no cheer, — would bring no good tidings. If God came into the world simply to tell us what God is and what is his ideal for humanity, the gospel would be the saddest message that could be conceived as delivered to the human race. As an athlete coming to a hospital merely to exhibit to hopeless invalids the glory of a vigorous manhood would add to their despair, so a perfectly righteous One coming into a world simply to show sinners how glorious is righteousness would enhance their gloom. Christ comes, not merely to show divinity to us, but to evolve the latent divinity which he has implanted in us. God has entered into the one man Christ Jesus, in order that through him he may enter into all men. Christ is a door, through which the divine enters into humanity, through which man enters into the divine. " Whom he did foreknow he also did predestinate to be conformed to the image of his Son, that he might be the first-born among many brethren."

Christ is not a man like other men, but mankind is to become like Christ. The tulip is not like the bulb, but the bulb is to become like the tulip. This is Christ's own declaration of the object of his mission. "I have come," he says, " that you might have life." How much? Life more abundantly. What kind of life? Eternal life. The life of God in the soul of man. The life that was in Christ. Life such that, when humanity is filled with it, his prayer will be fulfilled, " that they all may be one as thou, Father, art in me and I in thee, that they also may be one in us."

Christ, then, who is the secret of spiritual evolution, is also the type and pattern of that which will be wrought in universal humanity when spiritual evolution is consummated. The incarnation is not an isolated episode, — it is the beginning of a perpetual work. God is still Emmanuel, " God with us." God has not passed through human life, entering at one door and going out at the other; he has come into human life, and is gradually filling it with himself. Thus the Christ is a perpetual presence, an ever-living Christ. He is really in his church; his church is really his body; he is incarnating himself in humanity; and thus incarnate is still growing in wisdom and in favor with God and man. God is still a Word, still a speaking

God, still manifesting himself. He is entering into human consciousness, and the divine and human are inextricably intermingled in one divine-human consciousness. The end of evolution is a glorified humanity, a humanity in which God dwells. His tabernacle shall be with men. They shall be his children, and he shall be their God. This truth is written all through the New Testament; it shines on almost every page. Listen to Christ himself.

You shall be my disciples, my followers; shall take up my cross; shall do the works that I have done and even greater works than I have done. I send you into the world as the Father has sent me into the world: to teach as I have taught, to manifest God as I have manifested him; to suffer vicariously for others' sins, as I have suffered. The secret of my life shall be yours. Ye shall abide in me, and I will abide in you. You shall be as a branch engrafted on me, drawing as from my veins the life that animates me. You shall share my glory, the glory that I had with the Father before the world was; shall be with me where I am; shall be one with the Father as I am one with the Father. Paul takes up the same theme and writes it out with endless variation. Yet it is always the same theme. Righteousness in man is the righteousness of God, God's own right-

eousness, coming out of God's heart into human
hearts. We are partakers of the divine nature;
heirs of God — inheritors of his nature; joint
heirs with the Lord Jesus Christ; — having in
us the same spirit that was in him; holy as he
was holy; pure as he was pure. He is dead: we
are to die with him. He has risen: we are to
rise with him. Already we sit in the heavenly
places with him; reflecting his glory, we are
changed from glory to glory into the same image. There is scarce any title of dignity given
to Jesus Christ in the New Testament which is
not in a modified form given by the sacred writers to his followers. He is the Light of the
world, — we are lights in the world. He is the
only begotten Son of God, — we are sons of
God. He is the great High Priest, King of
kings and Lord of lords, — we are kings and
priests unto God. He is the eternal sacrifice,
— we are bidden to present our bodies living
sacrifices. God tabernacled in him, and tabernacles in us. In him dwelt the fullness of
the Godhead bodily, and we are bidden to pray
that, being rooted and grounded in love, we
also may be filled with all the fullness of God.
In brief, the Bible, starting with the declaration
that God made man in his own image, going on
to interpret God in the terms of human experience by the mouth of poet and prophet, and

finally revealing in the person of Jesus Christ an incarnate God dwelling in a perfect man, emphasizes the fundamental truth that in their essential natures God and man are the same, and points forward to the time when man, redeemed from the earthy and the animal débris which still clings to him, shall be presented faultless, because filled with the divine indwelling. Now are we sons of God, but sons at school and in process of education; then, when we see him, not adumbrated and incognito as we see him now, but in all the regal splendor of his character, and with all the justice and the purity and the love which constitute his divine glory, we shall be like him, and God will be in us, as in Christ, the All in all.

History is but the record of the process of this evolution of the divinity out of humanity. It is a continuous progressive change, from lower to higher, and from simpler to more complex. It is according to certain definite laws of the moral and spiritual life : and it is by means of resident forces, or rather a resident force, — the force of God in the individual soul; the force of Christ, — God manifest in the flesh, — in human society. Thus the church, Christian society, the individual, are all a strange intermixture of paganism and Christianity, in which Christianity is steadily, but surely, gaining the

victory over paganism. The church is partly
Roman imperialism and partly Christian brotherhood; but brotherhood is steadily displacing
imperialism. Society is partly pagan selfishness and partly Christian love; but Christian
love is steadily displacing pagan selfishness.
Theology is partly Christian truth and partly
pagan superstition; but truth is steadily displacing superstition. The individual man is
partly the animal from which he has come, and
partly the God who is coming into him; but
God is steadily displacing the animal. So,
whether we look at the individual, the church,
or society, we see the process of that spiritual
evolution by which, through Jesus Christ, men
are coming first to know God, and then to dwell
with him. Under the inspirational power of
the divine spirit their spiritual nature is growing stronger and their animal and earthly nature more subjugated; and when the end has
come, they will be heirs with God and joint heirs
with the Lord Jesus Christ.

In bringing this book to a close, I cannot
better sum up the conclusions to which I have
endeavored to conduct the reader, than by re-
defining some common theological phrases in
terms of evolutionary belief.

Christianity is an evolution, a growing revelation of God though prophets in the Old Testament, incarnate in Jesus Christ in the New Testament ; a revelation which is itself the secret and the power of a growing spiritual life in man, beginning in the early dawn of human history, when man first came to moral consciousness, and to be consummated no one can tell when or how.

Inspiration is the breathing of God upon the soul of man ; it is as universal as the race, but reaches its highest manifestation in the selected prophets of the Hebrew people.

Revelation is unveiling, but the veil is on the face of man, and not on the face of God ; and the revelation is therefore a progressive revelation, man growing in the knowledge of God as the veil of his ignorance and degradation is taken away.

Incarnation is the indwelling of God in a unique man, in order that all men may come to be at one with God.

Atonement is the bringing of man and God together ; uniting them, not as the river is united with the sea, losing its personality therein, but as the child is united with the father or the wife with the husband, the personality and individuality of man strengthened and increased by the union.

Sacrifice is not penalty borne by one person in order that another person may be relieved from the wrath of a third person; sacrifice is the sorrow which love feels for the loved one, and the shame which love endures with him because of his sin.

Repentance is the sorrow and the shame which the sinner feels for his own wrong-doing; when man is thus ashamed for himself, and his heavenly Father enters into that shame, as he has done from the foundation of the world, — a truth of God revealed by the Passion of the Word of God, — then, in this beginning of the commingling of the sorrow of the two is the beginning of atonement, the end of which is not until the penitent thinks as God thinks, feels as God feels, wills as God wills.

Redemption is not the restoration of man to a state of innocence from which he has fallen; it is the progress of spiritual evolution, by which, out of such clay as we are made of, God is creating a humanity that will be glorious at the last, in and with the glory manifested in Jesus Christ.

Finally: religion is not a creed, long or short, nor a ceremonial, complex or simple, nor a life more or less perfectly conformed to an external law; it is the life of God in the soul of man, re-creating the individual; through the individual constituting a church; and by the church transforming human society into a kingdom of God.